SECRETS EVERY C

THE SCRUM MASTER FILES

ANGELA JOHNSON

COMMITMENT

COURAGE

FOCUS

OPENNESS

RESPECT

**Copyright © 2021 by Angela Johnson
All Rights Reserved**

All rights reserved. No part of this publication may be reproduced, stored in a retrieval system, or transmitted in any form or by any means, electronic, mechanical, photocopying, recording, scanning, or otherwise, except as permitted under Sections 107 or 108 of the 1976 United States Copyright Act, without the prior written permission of the author.

This publication is designed to provide accurate and authoritative information in regard to the subject matter covered. It is sold with the understanding that neither the Publisher nor the Author is engaged in rendering legal, accounting, or other professional service. If legal advice or other expert assistance is required, the services of a competent professional person should be sought. Neither the publisher nor the Author shall be liable for damages, directly or indirectly, arising herefrom.

ISBN 978-1-7373574-0-7 (Kindle)
ISBN 978-1-7373574-1-4 (Print)
ISBN 978-1-7373574-2-1 (Audio)

Quantity discounts are available on bulk purchases of this book and the book can be completely customized for your organization to fit specific needs.
Contact us at: info@coleadteam.com

Cover art and illustrations by Chen Nir

First Edition

"Unfortunately, no one can be told what the Matrix is. You have to see it for yourself." – Morpheus[1]

---

[1] Wachowski, L., & Wachowski, L. (1999), *The Matrix*, Warner Bros.

Contents

About Angela Johnson	vii
Foreword *by Pollyanna Pixton*	ix
Foreword *by Esther Derby*	xi
Join Our Workshop	xiv
We Can't Adjust the Wind, but We Can Adjust the Sails	1
Why I Took the Red Pill	17
Scrum: A Different Way of Working	26
There are No Shortcuts: Shu Ha Ri	37
Case Study: Survivor Island	49
Case Study: Get Your Hand's Off the Team's Work!	66
Case Study: Do you Want Fries with That?	81
Case Study: Positively Neutral	95
Case Study: Your Lack of Faith is Disturbing	106
Case Study: Pardon my French	121
Final Secrets	136
Conclusion	149

About Angela Johnson

Angela Johnson has over 25+ years of experience working with teams and leaders in both project management and Agile environments. Angela started her career in technical support, quickly advancing to programming, database administration and project management. She realized that her passion was not in Gantt charts and status reports but in helping people work together more effectively within organizations. Becoming a Scrum Master enabled her to serve teams, Product Owners and leaders in companies adopting Agile and Scrum. In 2010, she founded her company to bring Agile education and coaching services to a diverse group of start-ups, Fortune 100 and 500 companies. Angela identified the best way to learn more about the highs and lows of Scrum adoptions was to immerse her own company into this way of working. In 2014 she renamed the company to Collaborative Leadership Team and began the same journey her clients were undertaking.

Collaborative Leadership Team uses Agile values and principles to manage the company and has the privilege of serving others in a variety of industries including: software, hardware, services, marketing and more. The breadth and depth of CoLeadTeam's experience extends beyond Scrum and includes Kanban, eXtreme Programming, Facilitation and Organizational Change for Business Agility.

Angela is a Training from the BACK of the Room (TBR) Certified Trainer, a Certified Scrum Trainer®, and a Certified LeSS Practitioner. She holds a Bachelor of Arts degree in Communication and Management from Hamline University and a Master of Business Communication from the University of St. Thomas. Angela lives in a western suburb of Minneapolis, Minnesota. Her greatest roles are Mom, Wife and Teammate. To read her published articles or listen to her podcast, please visit:
https://www.collaborativeleadershipteam.com/

Foreword

by Pollyanna Pixton

I met Angela about seven years ago when I was invited to a Scrum Alliance working group to develop Agile Leadership learning objectives. Being together in the group and being the only other woman, I got to know her well. We had great conversations around whether leadership could be taught or must be gained by experience. We concluded there could be guidelines, but great leaders come by it through their efforts to lead and how well they learn from those efforts. It was a lively discussion and other members of the group often disagreed with us!

After the group completed our work, I saw Angela at a conference and asked her to dinner. She shared that she could not drink much wine since she had to do her performance reviews. "Why are you doing them?" I replied. "Let them evaluate themselves. After all, how well do you really know their work?" At a later conference, I ran into her again and asked, "What did you do about the reviews?" "I let them review themselves! It went well but some were a little harder on themselves than I would have been."

Angela knows her stuff! She has learned leadership by doing and learning. In this book she not only shares her learning experiences but how she gained her insights, through her successes and her missteps. She understands the huge impact great leadership and coaching has on Agile success or failure. I've seen it many times. An organization fails with an Agile transformation due to poor leadership and coaching. While this book will be extremely useful for Scrum Masters, these ideas and experiences are applicable to all leaders and coaches.

She continues to learn, and I continue to learn whenever I have the opportunity to work with her. Angela walks the talk. Agile can be summed up in two words: continuous learning. That is Angela and now we have the opportunity to read her stories to continue learning.

What a great contribution to the Agile community!

Pollyanna Pixton

Co-author of The Agile Culture
Co-author of Stand Back and Deliver

Foreword

by Esther Derby

During the height of the pandemic, my neighbor, along with millions of others, decided to start baking sourdough bread. I cloned my starter and copied a basic recipe. We did a contact-free handoff via the back porch.

Later in the week after the recipe failed to produce edible bread, he called for advice. I asked questions to understand what went wrong. Here's what I learned. He'd measured *exactly* the amount of starter the recipe called for. He measured *exactly* the volume of flour. He added *exactly* the amount of water specified in the recipe. He followed the recipe *exactly*, and produced a brick, not a tasty loaf of bread.

What the recipe didn't say was that if you measure starter by volume, rather than weight, you need to stir it down first. Or that all purpose and bread flour contain different amount of protein which affects gluten formation. And that measuring flour by volume can produce variations of up to 20% in the weight of the flour. That older flour dries out and will absorb more water than fresh flour.

The recipe wasn't inaccurate nor incorrect. But, recipes, like training classes, focus on the stuff that is easy to write down and codify. Scrum training may address the events, roles, and rules of Scrum. This is called explicit knowledge. But that's not enough to be successful with Scrum or as a Scrum Master. For that, you need implicit knowledge, which is gained through experience. The good news is that you can learn from other's experiences, not just your own.

As Angela says, Scrum is simple but not easy. And being an effective Scrum Master is neither simple nor easy. You can't just follow the recipe and expect success.

Fortunately, Angela's book will help.

Angela draws on *principles* to suggest options. Principles, unlike recipes, apply to a broad array of cases. So, the reader will gain insight into specific situations, but also learn how to think about *any* situation they encounter.

Angela brings her years of experience, in life, as a project manager, technical trainer, technologist and, of course, as a Scrum consultant and trainer to this book. She dissects and examines problems that any Scrum Master may face—problems that can't be solved with a recipe. She suggests actions ... but not prescriptions. She's sharing the knowledge she's gained from deep experience, reflection, trial and error. It is the know-how and know-when that makes the difference between a loaf of bread and a brick. Or in this case, solving organizational problems rather than reciting recipes.

Esther Derby

Consultant, speaker
Author of 7 Rules for Positive, Productive Change
Co-author of Agile Retrospectives

Join Our Workshop

For more information, please visit us at:

https://thescrummasterfiles.com/

or scan the QR code

Chapter One

We Can't Adjust the Wind, but We Can Adjust the Sails

Before I was passionate about Scrum, one of my other passions was sailing. I loved racing as part of small, right-sized teams. There's something exhilarating about adapting to the current conditions of the wind and water. The motto of my favorite team was "without a plan, we have nothing from which to deviate." We would look up the lake and see that the breeze was filling in nicely on the right. We would formulate a starting line strategy accordingly and we'd be set! Then a few moments before the race start, the wind would shift direction. There would be no more breeze on the right side of the lake; it's all gone left. Time to adapt! Now, I don't claim to be a perfect sailor, but at least I didn't end up in the lake – most of the time – and once in a while our team even won races.

Chapter One

Scrum is a lot like sailing. The conditions are ever changing and demand that you stay in the moment to find ways to steer the group towards a successful outcome. It takes time to learn the ropes, but having achieved a level of competency, you can then focus on the external conditions, on what's happening all around you.

I didn't always sail – or work – in such an adaptive way. My technology career started over 25 years ago in a call center. I helped people "dial up" via a modem to an online database. That experience enabled me to learn software development as well as database administration. In the mid-to-late 90s I expanded my development and database skills by providing field support and training for data collectors. I converted flat-file data into relational databases. For some reason, I seemed to be able to explain these concepts in simple terms and was subsequently recruited to deliver database and development courses. I created a technical training practice to teach new developers and clients wishing to alter their own source code. Then one day my brain hit system failure.

I remember walking into Human Resources and saying, "I need a new job. I am seeing SQL statements in my sleep…I can't answer one more question about bind variables. Help!" And they turned me into a Project Manager. "What's that?" I asked. They believed that given my technical background I could effectively manage custom software projects. So, I began working towards my Project Management Professional (PMP)® credential through the Project Management Institute (PMI) and learning to follow practices described in the Project Management Body of Knowledge (PMBOK® Guide).

As I learned about this methodology, which many refer to as "Waterfall", it made no sense to me. I felt like an adult day-care provider checking up on people, and, like their administrative assistant, publishing status reports. Why couldn't these people talk to each other? Why couldn't they manage their own work? And why was I being asked to guess when other people would get things done and then held to those guesses as commitments?

In the early 2000s the organization I was working for brought in something new to one development area. They said it was called Agile. I read the Values and Principles that the creators of Agile had written in their Agile Manifesto. It wasn't about systems, filling in templates and passing off documents to one another, it was about talking to the customer and collaborating on

Chapter One

solutions real-time with each other. Aha! This seemed like common sense. At that point, I decided that this was the way I wanted to work going forward.

Today I introduce myself as a "recovering project manager". Recovery is absolutely the right description for me personally since it seemed like such a simple decision to change the way I did work. But really making that change was not easy. I had gone out into the world as a consultant and was finding that there was more work available - at that time - for project managers than for Scrum Masters. I did find organizations who said they wanted to use Scrum, but it was disheartening to learn that in practice they were still just using traditional project management with "Scrummy" language.

This seemed odd. Why would they do that? Because real change can be tough. Have you ever tried unlearning a process or breaking a habit that you acquired over time in order to replace it with something different? All that practice has made permanent, so it takes real effort to "unlearn" what has been learned … to recover from what you were doing previously.

In an effort to learn this new way of working I began using Scrum and Agile principles and practices everywhere I could, even if that wasn't something I advertised. As the way I personally did work evolved, I found that many of the companies I was working with weren't ready to make those same changes. They said that they wanted to "be Agile" but in practice would ask for traditional project management artifacts. Just because they went through the motions of standing up daily in short meetings didn't mean that they were changing the way they approached work with Scrum or that they were embracing Agile values and principles.

Looking back now, I realize when I was new to Agile, particularly Scrum, I was also going through the motions but hadn't internalized the "why" behind the mechanisms or their intended outcomes. When I was asked to work as a Scrum Master but to still deliver traditional project management artifacts under the premise of "transforming", it's obvious now that those were anti-patterns.

The ideas sounded good at the time, but in reality, they prohibited actual change and only served to become the new status quo. Instead of changing the way we were working in these organizations for the better, we were doing the same work two different ways. I struggled with these leaders who said that yes, they wanted to change but in reality, dug their heels in

Chapter One

and kept doing things the old way under the guise of "Agile" or "Scrum". Some of you may be thinking what I thought back then: when you need a paycheck, there's a fine line between challenging the status quo and pushing limits just enough to stay employed.

As I deepened my Scrum journey, I began to recognize these anti-patterns more quickly and I embraced the Scrum value of Courage in challenging that status quo. I was able to help my clients learn how to deliver business value more readily by understanding the meaning behind the Scrum framework.

I'm currently a Certified Scrum Trainer® and Business Agility Coach, teaching Scrum Masters, Product Owners, Developers, Leaders and Executives in their Companies how to deliver business value more rapidly with Scrum in all kinds of organizations (software, hardware, services, etc.). This is the fun part: helping others change the way they do work for the better. I'm also lucky enough to work as part of a team that works in an agile way. At Collaborative Leadership Team, we help individuals, companies and each other improve every day.

Our team's philosophy is not "those who can't do, teach." Our belief is "those who do, *should* teach."

Who better to learn agility from than a team who uses Agile? This also means that we have real learning, real client examples to bring to our teaching and coaching sessions. Students routinely tell us that these stories, these secrets, resonate and apply to the company they work in. Some insist that we must be, in fact, talking about where they work even when we are referring to a completely different company. The appeal of these stories seems to be universal. People can relate and see themselves in the scenarios. Many have shared that these very stories were instrumental in preparing them when they found themselves in similar situations after completing our courses.

Chapter One

This student feedback is one of the inspirations for this book. It's a collection of the most impactful stories and case studies from *my* experience; secrets I wish I'd known when I was a new Scrum Master. Don't worry! The names have been withheld to protect both the innocent … and the guilty! Great care has been taken to ensure that in sharing these stories no non-disclosures were violated.

With each story, you will find questions to work through in order to give you the chance to think about what *you* would do in these circumstances. These questions are another inspiration for *The Scrum Master Files*. This book is intended to help people learn to ask questions that get the conversation moving in a productive direction.

If you only learn one thing from reading this book, it should be that Scrum is about people. It's about working with other people, and that means you don't need a lot of product knowledge or technical knowledge to be a Scrum Master – just common sense and a desire to sharpen your people skills.

Scrum is simple…it is not Easy

This book is not about fixing other people. This book is about getting better at developing *your own* people skills as a Scrum Master. I believe that in order to be an effective servant leader, coach and a facilitator you must have great people skills. Improving people skills may involve drawing inspiration from psychology sources, theories of team development and many other references. Having great people skills is the secret to becoming a great Scrum Master.

Chapter One

This may sound simple since you already have a lifetime's experience of interacting with other people. That doesn't mean any of this is easy! What is going to be different is that, in your Scrum Master role, you will be paying attention to people in a slightly different way: more listening than talking, and you'll be intervening in a different way: more question asking than telling other people what to do. Your goal is continuous improvement of your people skills to enable higher performance in Developers, Product Owners and Organizations that you are coaching. And that will only happen by acknowledging the mistakes you make and adapting your behavior as a result.

When I was a new Scrum Master, moving away from Project Management, I didn't understand this. An example from one of my earlier mistakes involved a developer teaching me a deeper meaning about Scrum prescribing no specialized roles. Scrum currently describes a Scrum Master, a Product Owner and Developers. Developer isn't synonymous with any one activity that a singular team member performs. It's literally anyone on the team who is developing the product whether they are analyzing, building, testing, etc. This means no specialists and subsequently no heroes.

In project management people are temporarily assigned to a project, and sometimes multiple projects, based on a specialized activity they will perform: analysis, programming, testing, etc. When the end date approaches and cutting scope isn't an option, many organizations add "specialists" who can save the day. The Scrum Team I was serving seemed to be working well together. One person in particular struck me as a "hero". They consistently achieved and exceeded Sprint Goals, picked up extra work, paired with teammates teaching and sharing knowledge and testing others' work. In front of the entire team, I kept referring to this person as a "rock star" praising their efforts publicly.

This team member approached me privately and politely asked me to stop calling them out. They pointed out that phrases such as "rock star" and calling them out individually gave the appearance that others on the team weren't important and were somehow inferior. It detracted from building a sense of team.

This team member further explained that they were not offended, but offered that perhaps they were at a different place in their Scrum journey than I was which is why they chose to approach me privately and offer the feedback. This was an "aha" moment for me as a new Scrum Master. Even though I had good intentions,

Chapter One

my behavior was subtly undermining a sense of "team" by praising this one individual. That "aha" moment also told me I thought I was working in a new way but really, I was still behaving like a project manager and not a Scrum Master.

Scrum is a Framework, not a Methodology

Scrum is a framework that has been used to manage complex product development since the early 1990s. It is intentionally not prescriptive because tactically the process needed to build one product will not be the same as another. It is not a methodology. Methodologies tend to be more prescriptive. Scrum provides "guidelines" in the form of Values, Roles, Events, Artifacts and Activities and leaves the process to be determined contextually by the people doing the work. This will inevitably vary based on the company, the industry, the customers, the product, etc.

Warning: this book is not intended to be a beginner's book about the framework mechanics. I would like to think that you have read and understand the Agile Manifesto, have read and are familiar with the latest version of the Scrum Guide and have a functioning knowledge of Scrum and its five values: Commitment, Courage, Focus, Openness and Respect:

- Agile Manifesto: http://agilemanifesto.org/
- Scrum Guide: http://scrumguides.org/

Think of the Scrum Guide and the Agile Manifesto as the blueprint for bringing about change in the way work is done and you are ready to put the principles, values and framework into action. There are many good books and videos out there on Scrum 101, so I don't want to cover that ground in great detail. Because there are also many bad books and videos out there on Scrum 101 that provide inaccurate information and cause confusion, I will clarify elements from both the Agile Manifesto and Scrum Guide as necessary in the case studies to ensure that you can put your learning in context.

The Scrum Guide provides a basic framework which is where you should start if you are new to Scrum. Reading it prior to reading this book is essential. If you have not read it or the Agile Manifesto, hit the pause button and go do that now. You will be introduced to some new vocabulary, but don't let the Scrummy language get in the way. Scrum is easier *done* than *said*.

Chapter One

The stories in this book are not intended to suggest a magic bullet or a short cut. No such things exist when making the kind of structural and behavioral changes we are talking about. Due to the transparent nature of the framework and closer collaboration, Scrum tends to expose problems that already existed whether those are people, process, policies, product or organization structure. The case studies illustrate some of these impediments. Identifying the root cause and exploring possible solutions to these problems is also included.

There may be other possibilities ***not*** explored in this book that could be valid given the organization, the context and the people involved directly in a situation. The stories are intended to inspire Scrum Masters to shift their focus to behavior in order to coach higher performing Scrum Teams that meet their goals and deliver valuable products.

Another Warning: I love movies! You will find a number of movies quoted throughout the book that, for me, capture many ideas we try to convey about the nature of Agile or Scrum. Remember that famous scene in the Wachowski's (1999) *The Matrix?*[2]

Morpheus: "This is your last chance. After this, there is no turning back. You take the blue pill – the story ends, you wake up in your bed and believe whatever you want to believe. You take the red pill – you stay in Wonderland and I show you how deep the rabbit-hole goes."

All I have to offer you is the red pill, folks.

---

[2] Wachowski & Wachowski, *The Matrix*.

Chapter One

Chapter Two

Why I Took the Red Pill

When I learned to sail, I read books, went to seminars, took on-the-water classes and joined a crew willing to take on someone who was literally still learning the ropes. For any new skill needed for a new job, my learning acquisition has been the same: with each new technology, I combined personal research with classes and hands-on doing.

So, when I was asked to learn about Waterfall, I took the same approach. When I searched for courses, I discovered these weren't called "Waterfall" but Project Management or System Development Life Cycle (SDLC). Many advertisements included "learning the Waterfall methodology" as a learning objective. The credential a number of my project management peers were seeking was the Project Management Professional (PMP)® from the Project Management Institute (PMI).

Chapter Two

Not the "Waterfall Manager Professional" from the "Waterfall Management Institute".

As I went through project management training, I struggled with the concepts of "locking down scope" and "discouraging change". Change happens! How can you prevent it from occurring? The part that seemed reasonable to me was that if scope increased, then yes, costs and schedule would inevitably increase. But no customer ever wants to spend more money for things to take longer than originally requested.

In my research into the origins of why people kept calling project management "Waterfall", I found the work of Dr. Winston Royce.[3] As I read one of his papers, it seemed like someone was playing a really bad trick on me and many others. He was illustrating the famous picture that looks like a waterfall and stating **not** to do this! He mentioned that any process that doesn't take an iterative or incremental approach through the activities of analysis, design, build, test, etc. is "risky and invites failure".

---

[3] Royce, W. (1970), "Managing the development of large software systems", *Technical Papers of Western Electronic Show and Convention* (WesCon) August 25–28, 1970, Los Angeles, USA.

What?! The firm I was working for boasted in advertising that we used Waterfall for our custom software projects. When I tried to share Royce's paper with my peers, they honestly didn't believe what I'd learned. I was met with comments like "management knows what they are doing" and "this is the popular way to do work so all of those people can't be wrong."

Chapter Two

Copying Without Knowledge

Ah, but all of those people *could* be wrong. An opposing opinion came from the management consultant, W. Edwards Deming. He is best known for his work in Japan after World War II helping make industrial improvements by focusing on quality. Deming was critical of what was happening in the United States, especially when many believed they could just copy what Japan was doing. Without knowledge, he wondered, how would the U.S. know what to copy exactly?

This "copying without knowledge" phenomenon is one of the things that I believe popularized Waterfall. People looked at the diagram from Dr. Royce's paper that showed a series of descending hand-offs from activity to activity, made assumptions and took this as a prescription for their own organizations.

However, they failed to read the warnings about risk and failure that came with that famous diagram. Dr. Royce suggested iterating through the activities and taking an incremental approach to what was being built and keeping the customer continually involved as a better approach. It seems that nobody took the time to read this. They looked at the picture, made their assumptions and started copying.

Companies took this diagram and copied-without-knowledge to the extreme, putting in physical infrastructures to match the picture. Many segregated the activities that Royce described into separate departments. They created job titles that were synonymous with each activity. Then they put in management over each department and asked the people in these departments to hand off documents to one another.

The realization that struck me as a new Project Manager, was that my function was to run around and talk to all of these people and report back based on the "lost in translation" that was occurring with the segregation, hand-offs, and so on.

Simply copying the superficial aspects of something will not necessarily get you the desired results, and is unlikely to provide any understanding of what you are doing and why. Yet, for years we've seen this copying happen with Waterfall. A lack of accountability has been perpetuated by people staying in their box from Royce's picture:
"I don't build it – I just gather the requirements."

Chapter Two

"I just build what's in this document – I don't gather the requirements."

"I just test what's built – I don't build this stuff."

"I didn't ask for this – it's just what the I.T. department delivered."

By the time the customer gets to validate if the product meets their needs, it's too late. Too much money and time has been spent if they are unhappy with the result.

So why is waterfall thinking so attractive? It's a phenomenon that psychologists call 'cognitive ease'. A waterfall mindset doesn't require any deep thought processes, because we're already familiar with it – it's in every story that we have heard or read: it's just one step after another. "OK, work is the same so I'll use that same model to determine what I do." But that leaves out an important factor. One size does not fit all.

Scrum is Contextual

All Agile approaches, Scrum in particular, are contextual. They start with the customer in mind and enforce the iterative and incremental approach that Dr. Royce advised. However, the copying-without-knowledge phenomenon still seems to be happening with many newcomers who don't understand the intent of the Scrum Roles, Events, Artifacts, Activities and Values.

How can Scrum at Spotify be the same as Scrum at an insurance company? Are their business goals the same? I would hope not! Yet so many try to copy Spotify. They think they will get Spotify results by copying terms like 'guild' or 'squad'. It's impossible to copy another organization's journey. How would there be knowledge about the structural changes or behavioral changes made? What are the odds that the business goals and objectives are identical?

Copying without knowledge is alive and well in the Agile and Scrum community. All I have to say to prove this in a training class is that User Stories are not part of the Scrum framework. Even though students say they have read the Scrum Guide, say they understand what is Scrum and what is not, they are genuinely surprised. It demonstrates that there was no knowledge acquisition in determining where User Stories come from. There was no conscious conversation at their organization with an empowered Product Owner who owns the Product Backlog about whether they see value in capturing anything as a User Story. It's evident that people are blindly following others without owning

Chapter Two

their own knowledge or they are blindly following what's in a software tool that their company uses to "be Agile". What's the first value of the Agile Manifesto? If you do not know, please go read it now.

People imitate the outward appearance of doing work differently, but they are still using the same thinking and the same concepts that they have become accustomed to. One of the main differences between imitation and real understanding is that the latter provides you with some clues about what to do when things don't go according to plan. Only with real understanding can you inspect and adapt to get things back on track.

Another famous scene from the Wachowski's (1999) *The Matrix*:[4]

Morpheus: "I'm trying to free your mind, Neo. But I can only show you the door. You're the one that has to walk through it."

---

[4] Wachowski & Wachowski, *The Matrix*.

The Scrum Master Files

Chapter Three

Scrum: A Different Way of Working

After getting the hang of crewing on smaller sailboats, I decided to try big boat sailing. Some of the races on Lake Superior require a lot more preparation than small lake racing. One leg of a particular race could take anywhere between 20 and 30 hours. This requires the crew to eat, sleep and work in shifts. Imagine the gear that is needed for crew members, not to mention supplies for meals and drinking water in addition to the required safety equipment.

Not all big lake races require going offshore. Some races are held by setting a smaller course area for the purpose of completing as many races in a day as possible. On one such occasion the wind was particularly light. The boat's owner and skipper asked us to remove as much non-essential equipment from the

40-foot boat as possible. He was specific in wanting as much weight offloaded – including all of the toolboxes – because, given the light air, he reasoned, we wouldn't be needing those.

During the first race, the wind picked up speed. The skipper was just calling for a different head sail to be hoisted when the pin that attached the forestay broke. He turned the boat down wind, the main sail was eased and a halyard was run to the front of the boat – all in record time to keep the mast from coming down. This not only took great teamwork but quick adaptation by every member of the crew.

As the skipper called for a replacement pin from the toolbox, he was reminded that we had been instructed to remove all of the toolboxes. My position was in the pit – the center of the boat where all the lines that make sails go up and down run through. I was positioned at the top of the companionway to be able to effectively reach all of the lines for sail changes. I ducked my head down below and spotted the lock used to secure the boat's companionway when it was not in use. To me, the shackle looked like the same thickness as the forestay pin. Bringing the lock topside, I asked, "Will this do?"

Chapter Three

We quickly ran the forestay back and secured it with the lock and got back in the race. We made good time and even passed several boats. While sailing upwind, the skipper began complaining about the tiller extension sticking. "I'd ask for the WD-40 but I know that was probably in the toolbox," he said. Once again, I ducked below scanning the shelves for absolutely anything that would work. My eyes landed on a can of cooking oil spray on a small shelf above the stove. This was handed to the back of the boat and effectively used to loosen things up so that the tiller extension could once again move freely.

We didn't win that race. We were *not* in last place, either. This story, to me, is the epitome of agility. Yes, there was a plan, but when conditions changed, that plan no longer mattered. We knew that we had to adapt or withdraw from the race.

Many people believe that Agile or Scrum means having no plan or that the people doing the work do whatever they want to do. In reality, it's quite the opposite. Just like this sailing story, it means adapting despite the constraints and using what you ***do*** have to accomplish the job. It's looking at the art of what is possible.

Insanity: Doing the Same Thing Over and Over but Expecting Different Results

Now think about the work world. How many times do you hear people talking about sticking to the plan or simply refusing to adapt and marching to the original orders at all cost – even if that cost means everyone works unreasonable hours, sacrificing their personal

Chapter Three

time in an attempt to meet every scope item in the promised plan and the budget.

At the beginning of my courses, I ask participants to define the word different. Answers include: not the same; not normal; uncomfortable; change.

During the first day of the workshop, I need to refer back to the student definitions numerous times. Despite beginning with this exercise and framing up that Scrum means doing the work differently, people slip back into old thought patterns very quickly; they want to keep working the same old way with new vocabulary. They ask me to simply explain how to make Scrum fit into their organization as it has already been defined by Waterfall.

"I can answer that in two words," I reply. "It doesn't."

This gets back to my surprise (and frustration) at the number of organizations that say they want to use Scrum – "We want to go faster" – but fail to realize that this means actually changing the way they do work. This means changing structure and behavior. To go faster means looking at the work and then doing that work differently. People are working as fast as they can within the constraints of the current situation. Therefore, those constraints need to change or be removed. And that means changing the structure and consequently the culture of the organization. But that's tough – so they go for the perceived easy option of imitation. I like to say that these organizations can use all the Scrummy language that they want to, but that business value will not be delivered any sooner since they haven't changed how they're actually doing the work. Or worse, they keep working the old way and try to use Scrum in addition to project management on the same work.

Change is a part of the work. If you don't think differently, then you are likely to experience cognitive dissonance: the state of having inconsistent thoughts and beliefs especially related to decisions and attitude change.[5] You may be using new Agile and Scrummy words but if you haven't changed behavior, the intended goal (delivering value faster, higher quality, etc.) will not be met. This can lead to manipulating facts to justify where you were, or putting the blame on something or someone else for shortcomings. Ever heard someone say "We tried Agile, it didn't work" or

---

[5] Festinger, L. (1962), "Cognitive dissonance", *Scientific American*, 207 (4): 93–107.

Chapter Three

"We're using Scrum so now we have all of these problems"?

Another example of definition of insanity is organizations that say they want to use Scrum but won't let go of project management. Companies will continue to split people across two or three so-called Scrum Projects by singular skillset and then wonder why they fail to deliver any faster than before. They have done nothing in this scenario but add the Scrum events to several projects, time-slicing their people even more and using a bunch of new words that confuses everyone. It's no wonder those organizations foolishly say, "We tried Scrum and it didn't work." The truth is, they didn't really try Scrum at all.

The company has also given a built-in excuse to these people. When asked why Project A is not done, they will say because they were busy also trying to work on Project B and C at the same time. When people are 100% dedicated on the work that is highest in priority, there is focus, clear transparency and most importantly, no excuses.

There are no shortcuts or silver bullets for undertaking any kind of change. When organizations continue to "copy without knowledge" they rarely deliver customer value any faster or adapt quickly in the face of market changes. It's the same thing over and over but somehow, they expect it to be different because they said the word Agile or the word Scrum.

Scrum is based on empiricism. This means that knowledge isn't copied. Knowledge comes from experience and making decisions based on what's known and then adapting accordingly.

Empiricism: Transparency, Inspect, Adapt

The big lake sailing story is an example of empiricism in action. When the pin holding the forestay came loose, everyone could immediately see what had happened and we had to think on our feet. A quick inspection of the situation reminded us that we had removed all the non-essentials from the boat. Looking back, that could be considered a mistake, but that wasn't going to help us. There was no time to waste or any sense in assigning blame. Nobody talked about just following the plan; what mattered was dealing with conditions that had changed. We adapted and improvised with what we still had, skipper and crew alike.

Chapter Three

Empiricism is a key component not only of sailing but of life in general. Something everyone does empirically is learn to walk and learn to talk. As a toddler, there is transparency around you: you can see and hear what other people are doing. Walking and talking are not secrets! As you mimic their actions, the noises they make, you are imitating by inspecting and adapting. It takes time to achieve mastery. We learn what works and what doesn't work, by *experiencing*. We are constantly adapting our approach from what we tried last time.

This is one of the reasons I believe many who have an "aha" moment about Scrum say that it feels like common sense. It's an intuitive way of working, one that is better aligned with how we actually prefer to work and to learn – by doing. This way, we make better, informed decisions based on our experiences. When I perform assessments, however, I continue to be amazed at the lack of understanding about empiricism out there in the world of work. It's as if the waterfall-conditioning has calcified to the point where inspecting and adapting is no longer intuitive to people.

Empiricism requires making real-time course corrections. One of the keys to mastering Scrum lies in understanding the three pillars of empirical process control: transparency, inspection and adaptation.

The Scrum Master's job as servant leader to the Organization, to the Product Owner and to the Developers, is to teach how the roles, artifacts and events all provide transparency, inspection and adaptation opportunities; how to look at the work in a different way and get back on track if we aren't meeting goals and objectives.

The longer people have worked in a way that attempts to control change, it may take awhile for them to remember that change happens. The Scrum Master can continue to remind them that transparency about what's been learned, inspecting the possibilities and then adapting accordingly is what empiricism is about.

This reminds me of another scene from *The Matrix* in which Neo visits the Oracle for the first Time. He meets a boy holding a spoon as it appears to bend in the air:[6]

Spoon Boy: "Do not try and bend the spoon. That's impossible. Instead, only try to realize the truth."
Neo: "What truth?"

---

[6] Wachowski & Wachowski, *The Matrix*.

Chapter Three

Spoon Boy: "There is no spoon."
Neo: "There is no spoon?"
Spoon Boy: "Then you'll see, it is not the spoon that bends, it is only yourself."

Chapter Four

There are No Shortcuts: Shu Ha Ri

We live in a world in which we frequently seek short cuts to achievement and mastery. We do this even though we know that becoming highly skilled in some activity, such as sailing, violin-playing or championship tennis, takes hours of constant practice over a long period of time. When I was learning to sail, all the reading and classes meant nothing without actually practicing. Competing in races also meant adhering to the rules of the game; there are racing rules of sailing that must be respected. When they are not, there are penalties, just as with other activities and sports.

As people, we seem to yearn for The Secret because we believe that if we discover this key factor, we too will be able to achieve great things in a shorter time –

skipping the hard work. Think about all of those infomercials boasting instant and miraculous results if you simply buy and use their product.

There are no shortcuts. Mastery of Scrum requires putting in the effort, and learning from your mistakes.

Progress is never a straight line; life is not a Gantt chart. Waterfall is the illusion we have when looking back at what happened when all the failures have been edited out of the story. Because in reality, there were inevitable disruptions, diversions, dead ends, and retreats. Each time you revisit the Scrum basics, they will make a different kind of sense because you have changed, your understanding is better, and you will be able to relate your own experience to the theory. It's the same with the Case Studies in this book. Come back to them in a few months, having worked with your own teams and organizations, and you will be able to apply more of your own wisdom about what to do.

The Karate Kid

Many Agile and Scrum coaches refer to John G. Avildsen's 1984 movie *The Karate Kid* to illustrate the process of learning how to do things in a different way.[7] You've probably heard its most recognizable quote, "Wax on, wax off."

But there are other quotes from the movie that also strike a chord: "Walk on Road. Walk right side, safe. Walk left side, safe. Walk middle, sooner or later, you get squished, just like grape."[8]

---

[7] Avildsen, J. G. (1984), *The Karate Kid*, Columbia Pictures.
[8] Avildsen, *The Karate Kid*.

Chapter Four

In other words, you have to make a choice between working the old way with Waterfall, or working the new way with Scrum. Trying to work somewhere in the middle won't be effective – because eventually you will get squished.

The learning process – of martial arts such as karate – can be described as having three main stages: Shu, Ha, and Ri. This learning process also applies to mastering Scrum. Here's the way I think of the stages:

Shu: The basic facts that you need to know. The learner may not even understand why they are doing what they are doing but they are asked to execute the basics over and over and over again. Going through the motions with repetition is necessary to positively reinforce the new patterns and to let go of old patterns. In *The Karate Kid*, Daniel isn't aware of what he's learning or why he's doing what he's doing as he's painting the fence or sanding the floor. There are no shortcuts. The learner will not achieve Ha by skipping over the Shu experience.

Ha: The learner moves on from the mechanical application of the rules. "Aha! I get it now". At Ha, the learner connects what they are doing with the why. Working at the Ha level is more about the decisions you need to make having achieved understanding: Why are you doing this? What options do you have? How do you decide? When Mr. Miyagi begins sparring with Daniel, he has his "aha" moment! He understands why he needed to execute the mechanisms the way that he did at Shu – to block opposing moves.

Ri: The learner has transcended the basics. This is high level thinking: you can sum up situations quickly, know what to do and do it effortlessly. You are concentrating on the people, helping them find their own solutions and strategies, helping them acquire their own wisdom based on their personal experience. You have developed your own way of working. This will not be achieved by skipping the Shu or Ha experiences.

Learning is a dynamic process and you'll be working at all levels at different times. Each will take as long as it takes – there is no right or wrong or good or bad for how each person achieves understanding. So be careful to not assign some kind of false status value. Once you are actively demonstrating the basics of Scrum, it's time to think on a Ha level.

If you don't have a ready response, it's a good idea to go back to basics. This is why I focus on the basics in Scrum classes. That repetition, that discipline in Shu

Chapter Four

level is "conditioning" until understanding is achieved. At other times, you'll be able to size up a situation at first glance and have a pretty good idea of what to do in order to move forward.

How long it takes to become familiar with the Scrum framework will depend on the individual: how much practice they put in, how much reflective thinking they engage in to make sense of what happened, and in imagining how else they might do things in the future.

Scrum Masters need to be well-versed in the Shu aspects of Scrum and Agile – which means being totally familiar with the Scrum Guide and the Agile Manifesto. They also need to gain experience in working with Developers, their Product Owner and an Organization. This lets the Scrum Master know the kinds of things that are likely to happen, what is likely to happen if no intervention is made, and how the intervention they choose is going to be accepted (or not) by other people. Mistakes are part of the learning experience – your "waxing on process".

Stop Telling, Start Asking

One of the mistakes I made frequently as a new Scrum Master, was throwing up Scrummy language on people and telling instead of asking questions. Scrum Masters are servant leaders. They are intended to coach and guide not only teams of people and the Product Owner developing the product but also the Organization outside of the Scrum Team. This isn't accomplished through project plans or telling people answers. Coaches don't do the work for people. When have you ever seen a sports coach run out onto a field of play and rip the ball out of a player's hands? Or run out onto a track insisting on running a race for someone? Doing for someone prevents them from learning. It takes their own learning opportunity away and removes their accountability.

Scrum Mastery involves making observations and asking questions. When I was new to Scrum, I admit that I didn't understand this. My Waterfall Hangover was so strong that I believed I was supposed to behave as the project manager. The reality is that there is no project manager in Scrum. There isn't anyone assigned to first base in the American game of football either. That doesn't make it bad, that doesn't make it good. It means these are two different ways of doing work. It took me a long time to achieve that "aha" moment.

The best advice I can give new Scrum Masters is to stop telling and start asking. Stop telling people what

Chapter Four

you think they should do and start asking questions that lead them to their own conclusions. They will learn more and own the experience. It will also increase their accountability because they are bought into the solution and thus, the outcome.

The other part of that advice is to stop throwing up Agile and Scrummy vocabulary on people. Sometimes the words just confuse people and raise defenses as their brains try to determine if they are supposed to know what the terms mean. Scrum Masters may have the best intentions and not realize that a message can be conveyed using plain, simple language that everyone can understand to help situations and not make them worse.

The most unhelpful thing I hear new Scrum Masters say is "That's not Scrum" or a variation of it such as "That's not Agile". If you utter these phrases, be prepared for the response to be something like "So what?" Using Scrum isn't the organization's goal. Going Agile isn't the goal either. Organizations have goals and objectives about the products and services they offer to paying customers. Using Scrum or any Agile approach is a means to reach those goals and objectives. Scrum is about doing work differently. Effective Scrum Masters don't berate people who are trying to make these changes. They use powerful questions to help people come to their own conclusions and improve.

Here are some of the Do's and Don'ts I wish someone had shared with me as a new Scrum Master:

Do Ask...	Don't Say...
What problem are we trying to solve?	That's not Scrum! Or That's not Agile!
What is the goal or the objective we're trying to achieve?	We're/You're doing it wrong!
Are we meeting goals and objectives or not meeting goals and objectives?	We're/You're not doing it right!
In my/our current reality...	In the real world...

Wax on, wax off. Practice makes permanent. If your default behavior is to try to solve the problem for other people, document for other people, tell people what to do, you may have to work a little harder at pausing before speaking. In choosing to speak or to intervene, form a question that will enable others to own the solution or to arrive at their own conclusions. Use the case studies in this book as an opportunity to practice. In revisiting them, you may notice different details or think of new questions to ask in these scenarios which may help prepare you for similar scenarios in your reality.

The Trouble with Case Studies

As you try to change the way you do work and help others make that change, you may be asked to provide examples, stories or case studies about how others made this work. We live in a culture that thrives on stories. They can be an inspiration but beware trying to copy them as a prescription or a step-by-step playbook. Cognitive dissonance can creep in with people discounting any example and focusing on the countless reasons it doesn't apply to the situation at hand. Case studies are facts about someone else's journey. They can provide an example but there's no shortcut. Organizations will have to embark on the journey of change for themselves instead of "copying without knowledge".

The Case Studies I'm sharing with you are provided for inspiration and to help you to learn to think differently. The goal is to provide you with scenarios that will challenge you to improve your observation skills and question asking skills. With each story there will be questions for you to consider to become a more effective Scrum Master. The stories are not intended for anyone to try to copy as a recipe or a prescription.

It's helpful to have a notebook or to read the case studies with pen and paper readily available. Make note of your observations, questions you would ask in the situation and where you think an effective Scrum Master would or would not have intervened.

There are many organizations who say Scrum is the way they successfully now do their work.

There are many organizations who say "we tried Scrum – it didn't work".

What's the difference between those organizations?

The people involved and the choices they made. That's it!

It's like Morpheus says in *The Matrix*:[9]

---

[9] Wachowski & Wachowski, *The Matrix*.

Chapter Four

Morpheus: "Neo, sooner or later you're going to realize just as I did that there's a difference between knowing the path and walking the path."

Chapter Five

Case Study: Survivor Island

You're a contract Scrum Master working at an organization that has been using Scrum for the past year. Prior to this role, you were a traditional project manager. You are new to Scrum. Although you aren't a Certified ScrumMaster®, you have read the Scrum Guide, have taken a few classes and like that the Scrum Master role is the coach to the Organization, Product Owner and Developers. This will allow you to use your people skills rather than to be in more of an administrative position.

There are six Developers on the Scrum Team. The team members have been trained and are familiar with both the Agile Manifesto and Scrum Guide. Most are very mature in both Scrum and eXtreme Programming practices and seem in many ways to be a "dream team".

Chapter Five

Three of the team members are employees of the organization and the other three are contractors. The company has traditionally formed temporary project teams as its primary way of doing work. This area of the organization is trying Scrum but the larger company structure has not changed yet. As a result, the three employees all report up through different managers in the organization but their time is 100% dedicated to the efforts of this Scrum Team.

The first couple of sprints seemed to move along great. To the Product Owner's delight, the team achieved its goals and continued to pull in more work with each sprint. It almost seemed too good to be true. That's where the trouble either started or you now realized that all was not as perfect as it seemed. You started to pick up on the fact that one team member in particular was reluctant to identify and sign up for tasks at Sprint Planning and had little to say at Daily Scrums.

You engage the team member one-on-one to try to learn more. The two of you sit down over a cup of coffee and talk a bit about backgrounds and how you each got here.

"So, you've been working here for about five years now, is that right?" you ask.

"Yes. I am a Senior Developer so my boss volunteered me for this Scrum experiment. But by now I should be a manager," the employee said.

"How long has management been your goal?" you ask.

"Pretty much since the day I started. I've been in I.T. for so long I'm ready for something else. It seems like they keep promising it but it doesn't happen. I was told to be on this Scrum Team and if it goes well, I'll get the next management opening," the employee offers.

As the conversation comes to a close you wonder to yourself if this person is reluctant to take work based on seeing themselves as "senior" to the other team members and is just putting in their time until the opportunity for a promotion comes to fruition.

It's Sprint Planning Day. The Product Owner and Developers have agreed on the Sprint Goal. The PO was not able to stay for Topic 3 of Sprint Planning. Besides the Developers are comfortable reaching out to the PO should any additional questions come up as they break down Product Backlog Items into tasks creating their Sprint Backlog. Sticky notes are being written on and there is the usual flurry of activity with the team

Chapter Five

members identifying tasks, talking about working together on tasks, and so on. Only the "Senior Developer" is inactive and is sitting off to the side observing the activity.

One team member asks the Senior Developer to engage in task identification but they decline. Another team member notes that there are also issues reported by users that were pulled into the Sprint that could benefit from the Senior Developer's expertise. These issues needed root cause analysis so that the team can correct whatever in their process is causing the issues but then also fix them.

"Oh, no. I don't work on bugs. You all seem to forget that I'm a Senior Developer. Let the contractors fix the bugs," the Senior Developer says.

"What do you plan on contributing to the Sprint Goal?" you ask this team member.

"I'll think of something," comes the reply as they get up and leave the room.

The rest of the Developers turn to you and one at a time they each chime in with thoughts about the Senior Developer who left the room:

"We're tired of doing all of the work Sprint after Sprint while they play on the internet all day."

"Check their internet records, you'll see we're not making this up."

"We keep making the goal and exceeding it, so why do we even need them?"

"Think of what we could really do without them holding us back!"

"Let's just pretend like they're not part of the team going forward – because they have really voted themselves off this island."

Chapter Five

Waiving your hands, you're finally able to settle the team down, "Hold on. Don't you think we should try working with this team member or let me try to coach them before just voting them off the island?"

"You go right ahead and try," one team member says. "We have tried everything. We try pairing and they ignore us and check personal email right in front of us and start playing on the internet. They never take work and when we talk about what is next there is always some reason it's beneath them to work on."

Another team member says, "No. We're done. We are going to operate as if they aren't here because in spirit, they haven't been for quite a while now."

As you leave Sprint Planning you are pretty nervous about next steps. You know that a Scrum Master's job includes removing impediments to the Scrum Team's progress and improvement – regardless of whether the impediment is process, product or people-related.

You also know that a Scrum Master is a servant leader to not only the Product Owner and to the Developers but also to the Organization. Although you know who this Senior Developer reports to, you have never met that manager and are unsure of how much they know about what has been going on, let alone how much they know about Scrum.

Problem Identification:

As you work on the root cause of the problem in this scenario and begin to outline what you would do next if you were the Scrum Master, consider the following:

Chapter Five

Agile Manifesto Values and Principles

- Value: Individuals and Interactions over Processes and Tools.
- Principle #5: Build projects around motivated individuals. Give them the environment and the support they need, and trust them to get the job done.
- Principle #12: At regular intervals, the team reflects on how to become more effective, then tunes and adjusts its behavior accordingly.
- Other applicable values and principles you can think of?

Scrum Guide

- The Scrum values of commitment, courage, focus, openness and respect.
- The Scrum Team consists of one Scrum Master, one Product Owner and Developers; there is no hierarchy within a Scrum Team. No other titles are recognized within a Scrum Team.
- Specific skills needed by Developers are broad and will vary; Developers are always accountable for the Sprint Backlog, meeting Definition of Done, adapting daily toward the Sprint Goal and holding each other accountable as professionals.

The Scrum Master Files

- The Scrum Master is responsible for coaching the Scrum Team in self-management and working cross-functionally and helping those outside of the Scrum Team understand impediments to the Scrum Team's progress.
- The Scrum Master helps everyone understand Scrum theory and practice, both within the Scrum Team and the organization.
- Other Scrum Guide information you can think of that applies to this situation?

If it is helpful, read the case study again. Is there anything you would do differently if you were the Scrum Master in this scenario?

This isn't a "Scrum" problem. The root cause in this situation is a "people" problem. There may be things you identified to try differently than the Scrum Master in this scenario. It is evident that the Scrum Master attempted a conversation and was disrespected and the other Developers have also been disrespected. They can't be forgotten in this scenario and it's telling that they were willing to literally vote this person off the island based on what had been tried and how they had been responded to.

Chapter Five

It's noted that the Developers are familiar with the Scrum Guide. The guide is clear there are no roles or title other than Scrum Master, Product Owner and Developer on the Scrum Team. It's also clear that there is no hierarchy recognized within a Scrum Team. There's no "Senior Developer" or "Tech Lead". People are expected to work together to figure out what activities need to be performed and then execute these together. This doesn't mean dictating an organization's management structure or pay scale but Scrum does require structural change and behavioral change for successfully achieving goals and objectives. It begs the question if this organization's choices about incentives, management hierarchies, etc. are aligned with the way they are asking people to do the work or if they contradict the way people are asked to do the work. What is unknown is if these differences were acknowledged going into this experiment or if it's something that this company didn't even consider.

In order for a Scrum Master to effectively coach anyone (Developers, Product Owner or greater Organization on the Scrum Team's behalf) there must be respect for that person in the role. If someone isn't willing to be coached or isn't open to receiving feedback from the Scrum Master, it's unlikely that they will be effective.

What if we flip the scenario around and assume positive intent for the "Senior Developer"? Do we know for sure what direction they have been given by their manager? The Scrum Values are not one way. Is it respectful to them to have them in a situation or a role where they aren't happy either? This information isn't shared because the Scrum Master in the scenario had not yet engaged anyone outside the Scrum Team.

If the greater organization is not well versed in Scrum, it's unknown from the information provided if this Senior Developer has a manager that is giving them clear goals and objectives about the Scrum experiment. It's also possible this person is reading between the lines and making assumptions on what's expected of them to get the next management position.

Possible Solutions:

The next step for this Scrum Master is to engage the Senior Developer's manager in a conversation to learn the following:
- What direction, if any, has been given by management to the developer
- What promises, if any, have been made by management to the developer

Chapter Five

- What options, if any, are available to the developer if they don't want to stay on the Scrum Team and also what those options are if the developer does want to stay on the team
- What the manager's understanding of Scrum is; specifically, regarding behaviors expected on a cross-functional, self-managed team and how those will be communicated if the manager and developer agree that the developer will stay on this Scrum Team

There may be other things that you can think of to ask the manager. Engaging with them demonstrates respect for the current organizational structure but is also the appropriate level of escalation to address this situation. In conversation with the manager, next steps can be identified and pursued from there.

Evaluation:

When you initially read the scenario, did you focus on the Scrum framework? Many new to Scrum believe that the root cause has something to do with the mechanics of Sprint Planning. Yet others who don't understand that Developers work together on the tasks to accomplish a Product Backlog Item (PBI) within a Sprint will further misunderstand the scenario. It has nothing to do with "assigning stories" or "assigning PBIs". Scrum means working together in a "rugby-like" approach.

Sometimes people focus on pulling more work in or the Product Owner in this scenario. There is nothing wrong with pulling in more work that can be finished – that is desired with Scrum! Delivering more value. There is nothing in this case study that suggests the PO is contributing to the problem. They are engaged where they need to be and are happy with the results that are being produced. The PO is responsible for a successful product, not people and process; those are responsibilities of the Scrum Master.

Were your initial thoughts about how to solve the problem or how to make the Senior Developer comply or to try to "fix" this Developer in some way? Or were you focusing on details such as people being employees instead of contractors or vice versa? Scrum is about people working together. While there may be organizational nuances regarding how someone is paid, it doesn't really have any bearing on the chosen way to perform work. It may be a factor in how someone chooses to engage or is perceived but for this scenario, it only mattered to the "Senior Developer".

Chapter Five

From the scenario it seems like the Scrum Master knew that this part of the organization is committed to giving Scrum a try but that the company may not yet be working that way on a bigger scale. Principle #12 in the Agile Manifesto reminds us that we are seeking to continuously improve. With the benefit of hindsight, if the Scrum Master could go back in time, they may have all sorts of questions either in the interview process or shortly after starting about what this Scrum "experiment" means to the organization. They may have questions about the individuals involved and set up one on one conversations with everyone involved, not just the Senior Developer based on signs of trouble.

Although we do have a "people" problem in this scenario, it's impossible to change another person. Everyone has the gift of free will. Certainly, there are things in the environment that can be changed to bring about self-motivation such as the manager's expectations, goals and objectives given to employees, consequences of action or inaction within the organization, etc.

The Agile Manifesto value of individuals and interactions over process and tools reminds us that this is about people first – working together. Principle #5 talks about motivated individuals but that they need to be provided the environment and support that they need to get the job done. There are certainly successes being realized with this Scrum Team but there is more to be learned – especially if the organization is using this team as an experiment. The results of this experiment may be yielding a number of pieces of feedback but what we know for sure is that we can't arbitrarily put people together and expect them all to work well with each other. There may be hidden agendas, assumptions, attitudes, beliefs, personalities, etc. that need to be worked through.

A Scrum Master serving the Scrum Team certainly can engage this person's manager but depending on the outcome that is where their involvement would end. In order to be an effective, objective coach, it's generally not a good idea to get involved in those situations or to give any sort of opinion regarding them. If people perceive that a Scrum Master is not neutral and can affect their performance evaluation or can get them fired, they are unlikely to trust that person as their coach.

In this particular case, once the Scrum Master did engage the manager, the Senior Developer was moved to another part of the organization that didn't interact with this Scrum Team. The specifics about that move

Chapter Five

remain unknown and are not relevant. The remaining team members carried on delivering on their Sprint Goals and thriving as a team.

It reminds me of the scene where Morpheus is trying to explain what *The Matrix* is to Neo:[10]

Neo: "No. I don't believe. It's not possible."
Morpheus: "I didn't say it would be easy, Neo. I just said it would be the truth."

---

[10] Wachowski & Wachowski, *The Matrix*.

The Scrum Master Files

Chapter Six

Case Study: Get Your Hand's Off the Team's Work!

You're a Certified ScrumMaster® who has just accepted a job at a new company. In addition to your CSM® credential, you have prior Scrum Master experience with one previous organization. The new company has just begun their Agile journey and has chosen Scrum as the framework to adopt. They believe that Scrum will deliver results faster than the Waterfall process they used previously. They have identified a pilot team to do a proof of concept that consists primarily of people who have traditionally developed and tested software applications. The pilot team has had an initial two-day Scrum training course and is ready to begin working in Sprints.

Based on your previous Scrum Master experience, you know it may take a couple of sprints for any new team to figure out how to work together. Or potentially longer if old habits die hard and people fall back into the comfort of traditional roles. You are also aware that your job is to enable successful, accountable behaviors and not to become a crutch for the team.

The first Sprint Planning session was pretty rocky. The company thought adopting Scrum meant also choosing a software tool that they believed is necessary to "go Agile". Everyone at Sprint Planning had their laptops open and was staring at their screens. As the Product Owner described Product Backlog Items to pull into the Sprint, you facilitated conversations about how they would know that they achieved the Definition of Done. When it seemed that they reached consensus with the Product Owner and it was time to break the Product Backlog Items down into units of one day or less, Developers were still looking at their laptop screens and saying very little. When either you or the Product Owner tried to turn the conversation to the work breakdown their answers seemed limited to "Yes" or "No".

Prior to the next Sprint Planning event, one of the Developers asked to speak with you one on one. This

Chapter Six

Developer tells you that at the last company where they used Scrum, it was the Scrum Master's job to take notes and record all of the tasks identified during the Sprint Planning session. They suggested that in order for things to go more smoothly you should do the same for this particular pilot team.

You explain to the Developer that it's the team that owns their own work breakdown and recording of the Sprint Backlog. You further explain for the tasks to be meaningful and for the Developers to have a sense of shared ownership it's best that they own this process – they manage their own work. The Developer didn't seem convinced and mentioned that they needed to get back to their work.

It's the next Sprint Planning day. You walk into the team room and notice a new face. You introduce yourself as the Scrum Master. "Hi, I'm the team's Scrum Scribe," says the new addition.

"Scrum Scribe?" you ask raising an eyebrow.

A Developer chimed in, "We let the boss know that according to you Scrum means nobody writes anything down, so they hired a Scribe for us. The Scribe will be writing down all of the tasks and will enter any other notes needed into the tool for us."

You explain, "Scrum doesn't mean that nobody writes anything down. It just doesn't prescribe any one person who solely performs this activity." This explanation is met with silence. You probe deeper, "So the Scribe will be entering the tasks that all of you will be working on in the Sprint?" The Developers validate that this is the plan. You start to craft a response in your head about this not being the intent of a self-managed team or the intent of the Sprint Backlog. And then you decide to simply let the chips fall where they may.

"OK. Let's give it a try," you say and begin Sprint Planning.

The next two sprints didn't go very well. There was confusion about what the tasks for Product Backlog Items were. Team members rehashed Sprint Planning conversations before, during and after the Daily Scrum. They had to call the Product Owner over quite a bit for clarifications and didn't meet their Sprint Goal for either of the Sprints since the Scribe's arrival. Although there was quite a bit of information captured, the Scribe had done so based on the way they understood the

Chapter Six

conversations – all with no background, context or expertise on the Product.

Problem Identification:

As you work on the root cause of the problem in this scenario and begin to outline what you would do next if you were the Scrum Master, consider the following:

Agile Manifesto Values and Principles

- Value: Individuals and Interactions over Processes and Tools.
- Value: Working Software over Comprehensive Documentation.
- Principle #5: Build projects around motivated individuals. Give them the environment and the support they need, and trust them to get the job done.
- Principle #11: The best architectures, requirements, and designs emerge from self-organizing teams.
- Principle #12: At regular intervals, the team reflects on how to become more effective, then tunes and adjusts its behavior accordingly.
- Other applicable values and principles you can think of?

The Scrum Master Files

Scrum Guide

- The Scrum values of commitment, courage, focus, openness and respect.
- The Scrum Team consists of one Scrum Master, one Product Owner and Developers; there is no hierarchy within a Scrum Team. No other titles are recognized within a Scrum Team.
- Specific skills needed by Developers are broad and will vary; Developers are always accountable for the Sprint Backlog, meeting Definition of Done, adapting daily toward the Sprint Goal and holding each other accountable as professionals.
- The Scrum Master is responsible for coaching the Scrum Team in self-management and working cross-functionally and helping those outside of the Scrum Team understand impediments to the Scrum Team's progress.
- The Scrum Master helps everyone understand Scrum theory and practice, both within the Scrum Team and the organization.
- The Sprint Backlog is a plan by and for the Developers. It is a highly visible, real-time picture of the work that the Developers plan to accomplish during the Sprint in order to achieve the Sprint Goal.
- Other Scrum Guide information you can think of that applies to this situation?

Chapter Six

If it is helpful, read the case study again. Is there anything you would do differently if you were the Scrum Master in this scenario?

As with most impediments that occur when adopting Scrum, this is another "people" problem. The root cause in this situation doesn't have anything to do with the organization or the framework. The Developers were not demonstrating openness to doing work in a different way. They were seeing work through their old, Waterfall lens where one activity had a separate title. They had grown used to other people writing things down for them and not owning their own work.

Scrum's origin in the Harvard Business Review article "The New New Product Development Game" describes people doing work in a "rugby-like" approach.[11] Developer doesn't refer to software development but anyone that is working on developing the product. If you conduct simple online searches in science, psychological science and adult learning, you'll find all kinds of research that indicate people who write things down are retaining and learning more than those who are not.

---

[11] Takeuchi, H., & Nonaka, I. (1986), "The New New Product Development Game", *Harvard Business Review*, 64, 137-146.

In *Informal Learning* by Jay Cross, such workplace practices are critiqued.[12] People don't think about learning to learn. Cross maintains that taking notes is a valuable form of processing information and increasing the likelihood of understanding and remembering the subject matter. Think about the scenario just described. Does this organization really want a "Scribe" knowing the most about their product rather than the people building it?

There may be things you identified to try differently than the Scrum Master in this scenario but this one decided that failure would be the greatest teacher. Trying a few Sprints with the Scribe didn't make things better, it made them worse! Sometimes just running an experiment and inspecting the outcome is better than engaging in debates or arguments over an issue.

It's a bit of a Waterfall Hangover when people are not willing to write things down for themselves or believe that there are named roles who "take notes" or document. These people may have grown accustomed to having someone else do this for them, but that's not empowerment, that's learned helplessness. Leaders will

---

[12] Cross, J. (2007), *Informal learning: Rediscovering the natural pathways that inspire innovation and performance*, Pfeiffer/John Wiley & Sons.

Chapter Six

say they want accountability yet one of the first things they do is take that accountability away by letting the people doing the work off the hook by having someone else responsible for writing. Scrum can increase accountability if used as intended. The Sprint Backlog is the way the Developers manage their own work. Hence the title "Get Your Hands Off the Team's Work".

What is also unknown is why the team engaged the manager for a solution without talking to or involving the Scrum Master. It was clearly a surprise to them that a Scribe was hired. If Scrum is the new way that has been chosen to do work, why leave the Scrum Master out? Why take one Developer's perception who used Scrum at another organization that Scrum means the Scrum Master takes notes?

If the greater organization isn't well versed in Scrum, it's unknown from the information provided if the manager who approved the procurement of a Scribe understands that Scrum isn't something you do in addition to work. Scrum is a different way to do the work. Which means change.

Possible Solutions:

The Scrum Master in this scenario chose to run the experiment and see how the next few Sprints would go. Now that there are data points to leverage, it's time for next steps. The Scrum Master needs to engage the manager in a conversation to learn:
- What problem was presented and why hiring a Scribe was the solution

Chapter Six

- Were other solutions proposed?
- What the manager's understanding of Scrum is specifically regarding the empowered ownership the team is intended to have over their own work

It's also helpful for the Scrum Master to share the free, official Scrum Guide with the manager so that they can learn for themselves what is intended with Scrum. The Scrum Master also can share the outcome of having the Scribe present in the way of:

- Wasted time in rehashing conversations (which means wasted money)
- Wasted money in an additional role that isn't needed or intended
- Even more wasted time and money for the product given that the Sprint Goals went unmet for the next few Sprints
- Engaging the Product Owner to further explain the negative outcomes to the product's release schedule and overall budget

There may be other things that you can think of to ask the manager. Engaging with them demonstrates respect for the current organizational structure but also engages the appropriate level to address this situation. In conversation with the manager, next steps can be identified and then pursued from there.

There is also an opportunity in this instance for the Scrum Master to educate the Developers on the intent of Sprint Planning and that it's a hands-on, working session. This could be at the Sprint Retrospective or a session on its own. There is also an opportunity to educate them on the intent of the Sprint Backlog and how the Developers, not someone else, use it to manage their own work.

Evaluation:

When you initially read the scenario, what did you focus on? Many new to Scrum believe that the root cause has something to do with team members not knowing how to "capture requirements". That isn't the root cause in this case. Sprint Planning is also not the first time the Developers and the Product Owner are discussing the Product Backlog items. There would have been at least one round of Refinement on the item if not more for them to discuss it. If it's determined that team members are not "good" at writing down their work, how do you think people get better at something? That's right! By doing it ... not by having someone else do it for them.

Were your initial thoughts that as Scrum Master you somehow needed to get the Scribe up to speed on the

Chapter Six

product? That would have meant skipping any question asking to get to the root cause and also making the assumption that this is the only solution or the solution that will be staying in place.

Or were you focusing on a manager solving the problem and telling yourself that this is the way things will be then. The Scrum Master has responsibility outside the Scrum Team to the greater Organization. Not only to help guide and educate but to also escalate for the removal of impediments. In this instance, even if the manager thought they were doing the right thing, by imposing a solution, did they empower the Developers or disempower them? How about taking away the Developers accountability and their learning opportunity? Some ideas might seem positive when they are first mentioned but a Scrum Master has responsibility to ensure people are talking to each other and that all possible outcomes or consequences are explored and thought through.

Let's not forget that the Product Owner, not a separate manager, is responsible for the budget, the scope and the timeline of the overall product. A Product Owner's decisions are respected by the entire organization according to the Scrum Guide. There's no mention in the scenario of the Product Owner being consulted about impacts to their product as a result of what's going on. This is another coachable opportunity for the greater Organization. Old habits die hard. The Scrum Master as Coach will need to help people understand this new way of working with Scrum, its events and artifacts as the way we do work, until it becomes second nature for everyone.

In this particular case, once the Scrum Master did engage the manager and the Product Owner, the Scribe's services were no longer required. The Developers learned to break down work at Sprint Planning which enabled transparency and impediment inspection at Daily Scrum. This allowed for earlier adaptation and the Scrum Team had its "aha" moment about Empiricism. They understood why their initial Scribe solution was not as impactful as getting their hands on their own work.

In *The Matrix* Neo is given many training exercises. This case study reminds me of such a training simulation about the Matrix itself where people are seen walking on a sidewalk along a busy street:[13]

Morpheus: "You have to understand most of these people are not ready to be unplugged. And many of

---

[13] Wachowski & Wachowski, *The Matrix*.

Chapter Six

them are so inured, so hopelessly dependent on the system that they will fight to protect it."

Chapter Seven

Case Study: Do you Want Fries with That?

You're the Scrum Master of a newly formed Scrum Team. This is your first Scrum Master role. Prior to saying yes to this experiment, you worked as a project manager for just over ten years. Everyone, including you, is fresh out of training on Agile and Scrum with just one Sprint completed. There's a Refinement conversation planned and the Developers have asked a Database Administrator (DBA) and an Enterprise Architect to sit in on the session to provide input. You have asked the organization's Agile Coach to observe this activity and to provide feedback.

Refinement seems to start off pretty well. The Product Owner (PO) initially refined Product Backlog

Chapter Seven

Items (PBIs) with stakeholders and customers and was prepared to share information on the highest valued items on the Product Backlog. You kick off the conversation inviting the Developers to ask the PO questions as you settle in to capture the results of their conversation.

For one of the high valued items, the PO explains, "What we really need for this item is just one screen. The eight screens that we currently have are confusing and take too long to navigate. I need you to keep all the existing fields but remove duplicates and put everything onto one screen. Use a grid if you have to but get it on one screen."

A Developer asks, "Do you want to validate data at the field level each time you navigate to the next field? Or is it ok for us to validate the data after you are all done entering data into this proposed single screen?"

The PO thinks for a moment and says, "Validating at the field level would be great! Let's do that."

The DBA and the Enterprise Architect audibly gasp as Developers begin mumbling to each other and other side conversations occur. The team member who raised the issue says, "According to Scrum the PO gets what they want. So, this is the way it has to be."

As the Scrum Master, you have been taking detailed notes during this discussion typing them into software the company has mandated for its Agile adoption. The side conversations are still going on which you think gives you time to finish your notes. A long moment of uncomfortable silence followed. You didn't realize the Agile Coach had been trying to get your attention, but you turn back to your typing in an effort to capture everything you thought you heard.

The Agile Coach broke the silence, "Sorry. Unhappy Coach in the room." The coach turned to the visiting Architect and Database Administrator who had been mumbling to each other and said, "Please share your concerns with the whole group here." They started talking about throughput, CPU usage, database commits, when the Coach interjected "Please – in very plain words."

They looked at the Product Owner and said, "If we validate data as it's entered in the form it will be very, very slow."

Chapter Seven

"Slow? I didn't ask for slow," said the PO "I am just fine having it happen when the 'ok' button is clicked at the bottom of the form." A long moment of uncomfortable silence followed.

"I thought that the PO gets what they want according to Scrum," offered a Developer.

"Here comes the *Spiderman* speech folks," the coach said. "With great power comes great responsibility."[14] You are professionals. You are a collaborative part of this process. That means it's your job to educate the PO on the pros and cons of some of these usability or design choices. You are not order takers – you are collaborative partners."

The Agile Coach continued facilitating the conversation through agreement on criteria to meet Definition of Done. You wrap up your note taking and approach the Agile Coach and ask, "Why did you jump in there?"

With a tilt of the head, the Agile Coach gives you a quizzical look and asks, "Why didn't you?"

---

[14] S. Lee., & S. Ditko. (1962), "Spider- Man", *Amazing Fantasy*, No. 15: p. 13

Problem Identification:

As you work to identify the root cause of the problem in this scenario or what you would do differently if *you* were the Scrum Master, consider the following:

Agile Manifesto Values and Principles

- Value: Individuals and Interactions over Processes and Tools.
- Principle #4: Business People and Developers must work together.
- Principle #5: Build projects around motivated individuals. Give them the environment and the support they need, and trust them to get the job done.
- Principle #11: The best architectures, requirements and designs emerge from self-organizing teams.
- Other applicable values and principles you can think of?

Scrum Guide

- The Scrum values of commitment, courage, focus, openness and respect.
- The Scrum Team is responsible for all product-related activities.

Chapter Seven

- The entire Scrum Team is accountable for creating a valuable, useful Increment every Sprint.
- No one else tells the Developers how to turn Product Backlog Items into Increments of value.
- The Scrum Master coaches the Scrum Team in self-management and helps them understand the need for clear and concise PBIs.
- Facilitates collaboration as requested or as needed.
- Other Scrum Guide information you can think of that applies to this situation?

If it's helpful, read the case study again. There may be things you identified to do differently than the Scrum Master in this scenario but the Scrum Master *is* the problem here! Scrum mastery has nothing to do with taking notes for other people. Neutral facilitation also doesn't mean leading, that's the Product Owner's job. In this scenario an objective facilitator was necessary to intervene to help clear up the confusion that was obviously taking place.

The PO doesn't "get what they want and that's the way it is". Product Owners aren't dictators or all-knowing beings. Yes, they can ask for what they want but they take input and collaborate with the Developers. The Scrum Team is comprised of a PO, a SM and

Developers. There's no hierarchy or "us" vs. "the PO" intended in Scrum.

Stakeholder input is welcome. A Refinement conversation doesn't have to be closed to those who are not on the Scrum Team. Having an Architect, a Database Administrator or any Subject Matter Expert in the conversation is not the problem here. In fact, if they hadn't been there to react the way that they did, the pros and cons of the PBI may have gone unmentioned which could have resulted in the item not getting to done in the Sprint that it gets pulled into.

Getting work done effectively occurs when people are motivated, creatively thinking and asking great questions. The Scrum Master and Developers are in 'order taker' mode as if they are taking dictation from the PO – hence the title *Do You Want Fries with That?* The Scrum Master is so busy taking dictation they completely miss the teachable moment to clear up misconceptions about Scrum. Team members are assuming things about the framework that just aren't true.

The Scrum Guide points out that the Developers are empowered professionals which means having responsibility for how to turn the PBI into a valuable

Chapter Seven

Increment. A professional would explain to the PO the various solution approaches and the pros and cons associated with each of those choices to help the Product Owner understand why they chose the solution that they did.

An Agile Coach isn't a role on a Scrum Team. The Scrum Master is the Coach to the Developers the PO and the greater organization. When a SM is newer, some organizations engage an external coach for a few Sprints to help get the Scrum Master up to speed. But that additional "Agile Coach" would not be needed after a few Sprints if the SM is starting to perform the role as intended.

It's ok - and expected - for collaboration on the PBI to occur during Refinement. There's no one role in Scrum that has the singular responsibility of writing down what is agreed to or what is said. When a Scrum Master assumes that they are the note-taker, they not only miss exactly what their job is intended to be, they create several additional dysfunctions. If their focus is looking at a page while writing – or worse, looking at a screen they are typing into – they are inevitably missing the cues that tell them, "this is a coachable moment" or "this moment needs active facilitation to get it unstuck."

The Agile Coach, in this case, identified the misunderstanding and confusion and jumped into neutral facilitation mode to clear this up. They also addressed the teachable moment that the Scrum Master missed because they were busy typing.

Recall the brain science tip shared earlier; the people who write the most learn the most. The best people to write down what they understood are the very people

Chapter Seven

who have to execute that work. The Scrum Master in this scenario is not only missing the facilitation and coaching opportunities, but is taking the Scrum Team's learning opportunities away from them and also their accountability.

Ask yourself: are you empowering someone when you do a task for them – like taking their notes – or are you disempowering them? Will they see you as a coach? Or as a secretary?

Possible Solutions:

The next step for this Scrum Master is to engage the Agile Coach in a conversation to:
- Listen to what the Agile Coach observed about what was happening in the room
- Understand how typing for everyone wasn't adding value, helping or guiding the stakeholders and Scrum Team
- Identify ways to improve in Scrum Mastery
- Learn from the mistakes made in this session to prevent making them, if possible, in future opportunities for the SM to serve the Scrum Team and others in the organization

It may be the case where the Scrum Master in this scenario just doesn't know what they are intended to do as a Scrum Master. They could have too many years of Project Management behavior to "unlearn". Another possibility could be that they do not want to be a Scrum Master. There may also be other things that you can think of but really the only possible solution starts with the Scrum Master.

Evaluation:

When you initially read the scenario, what did you focus on? Many new to Scrum believe things that are not true such as a DBA and an architect shouldn't be allowed in a Refinement conversation. Yet others who read this scenario will assume what the Developer said about the Product Owner getting what they want is true. They will then go down the path of thinking the PO wasn't ready and prescriptively try to implement something that doesn't exist in Scrum such as Definition of Ready that would prevent people from talking and would make the misunderstandings in this scenario so much worse.

Some will read the scenario and think the Product Owner should not have refined the PBI with stakeholders first. That is perfectly ok and ideal in a

Chapter Seven

Scrum adoption. If it's decided at that level not to pursue a PBI, the Developers' time doesn't need to be wasted on something that will be abandoned. We encourage business people and developers to interact yes, on the PBIs that will be pulled into a Sprint.

Yet others new to Scrum think the SM is somehow the same as a project manager and should take notes.

No Agile method prescribes "a note-taker". Individuals and Interactions over Processes and Tools. Motivated Individuals. The Developers own and manage their own work. Recall that Scrum requires structural change but also behavioral change. The Scrum Master is the coach that helps people make those changes. Which is hard to do if they aren't paying attention to those needs.

In this particular instance, I was the Agile Coach asked to observe. When the SM asked why I had intervened and I asked, "Why didn't *you*", I was being serious. I was trying to get the SM to have an "aha" moment. The person in question was not only unwilling to be coached and unwilling to stop taking notes for everyone, they went even further with producing charts and graphs and trying to be the stakeholder manager when that is the Product Owner responsibility in Scrum.

The Scrum Master in this case study did have an "aha" moment but it was that they didn't want to be a Scrum Master after all. They accepted a project management role with a different company and the company in this scenario found a new SM who wanted to embrace the role as intended.

Anyone else thinking of the scene from *The Matrix* where Neo is late and called in front of the boss?[15]

Boss: "The time has come to make a choice, Mr. Anderson. Either you choose to be on time from this day forth or you choose to find yourself another job."

---

[15] Wachowski & Wachowski, *The Matrix*.

Chapter Seven

Chapter Eight

Case Study: Positively Neutral

You're a new Scrum Master at an organization that has decided to use Scrum for a number of initiatives. Training was held for all Scrum Masters, Product Owners and Developers for these pilot initiatives in order to start things off on the right foot.

In order to share learnings across the various newly formed teams, you and the other Scrum Masters have formed a Community of Practice (CoP). This Scrum Master CoP meets every few weeks to share ideas, experiences and coaching tips to improve how you serve the Developers, the Product Owners and the greater Organization.

As a result of the recent CoP discussion, the group decided to take turns observing each other's Sprint

Chapter Eight

Planning events and providing feedback to one another following these sessions. You offer to observe a fellow Scrum Master's Sprint Planning that is scheduled for the next morning since your own team's planning event is not until the afternoon.

You arrive the next morning as an observer for the Sprint Planning event. You take a seat slightly behind the Scrum Master so that you don't draw attention to yourself. The Scrum Master explains your presence pointing out that your role is only as an observer for this event.

Sprint Planning begins with the Scrum Master validating the available Capacity for the Developers based on upcoming holidays, vacations and other calendar conflicts in relation to the historical work completed in prior Sprints.

Topic One of Sprint Planning goes smoothly with the Developers and the Product Owner agreeing upon a Sprint Goal. For Topic Two, there is good discussion and agreement on the Definition of Done and which Product Backlog Items (PBIs) are needed to meet the Sprint Goal.

Topic Three of Sprint Planning is underway with Developers creating their Sprint Backlog and discussing solution approaches to accomplishing the agreed upon PBIs. Two team members disagree over one of the solution approaches and their voices begin to get louder with each passing minute.

Tensions begin to increase with remaining team members and Product Owner nervously exchanging glances but nobody dares interrupt the heated debate. The Scrum Master silently listens, turning their glance back and forth between the team members as each interjects.

Both team members' faces are very red, their fists are clenched and you believe a fight may break out at any minute.

You lean over to the Scrum Master and whisper "Scrum Master, get in there…"

The Scrum Master turns to you and says "Shh. I'm being neutral."

Chapter Eight

Problem Identification:

As you work to identify the root cause of the problem in this scenario or what you would do differently if *you* were the SM, consider the following:

Agile Manifesto Values and Principles

- Principle #5: Build projects around motivated individuals. Give them the environment and the support they need, and trust them to get the job done.
- Principle #10: Simplicity – the art of maximizing the amount of work not done – is essential.
- Principle #11: The best architectures, requirements and designs emerge from self-organizing teams.
- Other applicable values and principles you can think of?

Scrum Guide

- The Scrum values of commitment, courage, focus, openness and respect.
- The Scrum Team is responsible for all product-related activities.
- The entire Scrum Team is accountable for creating a valuable, useful Increment every Sprint.
- No one else tells the Developers how to turn Product Backlog Items into Increments of value.
- The Scrum Master coaches the Scrum Team in self-management and helps them understand the need for clear and concise PBIs.
- Facilitates collaboration as requested or as needed.

Chapter Eight

- Other Scrum Guide information you can think of that applies to this situation?

If it's helpful, read the case study again. The Developers having communication challenges and a disagreement is one issue. The larger issue, once again, *is* the Scrum Master. What is missing is Active Facilitation. The Scrum Master in this case somehow is equating *neutrality* with *doing nothing*. Hence the title Positively Neutral.

While neutral facilitation isn't necessarily about taking notes for everyone, it doesn't mean staying silent and not doing anything. Facilitators help everyone achieve their goal. In this case, consensus on how the PBIs in the Sprint will be accomplished. From the information provided, there are clear visual cues and verbal cues that let everyone know tension was building and a conflict was underway. In this scenario a neutral, active facilitator is needed to break up the tension, call for a break and certainly to help achieve some sort of consensus.

What of the visiting Scrum Master? They're in an awkward position. Yes, their instincts were spot on that intervention is needed but it had been made clear to all they were in observation-mode only. Would it be respectful to then jump in as facilitator? Perhaps simply calling for a break is something the visiting Scrum Master could have done as a way to chat one on one with this Scrum Master, ease the tension and not give the appearance that they were undermining anyone.

The good news is that the Scrum Masters have established a Community of Practice in order to learn together and to learn from each other. If we go back to the basics, or Shu-level thinking, there are good reminders from the Agile Manifesto and the Scrum Guide that can help. There's an opportunity for the Scrum Master to work on their active facilitation skills. Neutrality is important so the Scrum Master doesn't take sides. As facilitator, they could also have called for each person to list their thoughts and then called for discussion on pros and cons and eventual consensus. There are more than these two Developers on the team. The Scrum Master can always appeal to the whole team of Developers. Perhaps they have questions or would invite clarifications from the Product Owner that may help. In this scenario, the other Developers and Product Owner may have felt uncomfortable in joining the discussion given the tension and conflict exhibited by two of the Developers.

Chapter Eight

Possible Solutions:

The next step for this Scrum Master is to:
- Call for a break
- Ask the visiting Scrum Master what their observations were and for more information on why they knew it was time for someone to intervene
- In resuming Topic 3 of Sprint Planning, ask each person to lay out the possible solution ideas and have the Developers as a team decide
- It's important to give each person a chance to be heard and for their teammates to ask any questions or potentially come up with yet another option that may work out for the better
- If there is no working agreement yet, since it's noted that everyone is newer to using Scrum, the Scrum Master can facilitate the creation of one
- A critical element of a working agreement is how the team will reach consensus when there are differing opinions

Another technique the Scrum Master could use is dot-voting to help the Developers quickly reach consensus on the proposed solutions.

Disagreements will happen. It's not realistic to think that everyone on every team will get along perfectly all of the time. When emotions and tensions flare, a calm, neutral Scrum Master is needed to get things back on track. So many Scrum Masters miss this because they have their noses buried in a tool, a laptop or their phone. They need to be tuned in to what is happening in the discussion and assist when needed.

Evaluation:

When you initially read the scenario, what did you focus on? Many new to Scrum believe things that aren't true such as the Scrum Masters having a Community of Practice and inviting someone to observe is part of the problem. Yet others who read this scenario will assume the Product Owner should be the one to decide on the "how" or the technical solution. The Scrum Guide is clear that for Topic Three of Sprint Planning, no one can tell Developers how to turn Product Backlog items into Increments of Value. Which is why both a neutral facilitator and team agreements on making decisions once options are discussed are helpful.

Another common myth is that the Scrum Master should not be present when PBIs are being broken down into the technical tasks. Neutral facilitation isn't leading or dictating. If interpersonal conflicts happen or people are just misunderstanding each other, a

Chapter Eight

facilitator can help get things back on track or keep them there in the first place. Being a Scrum Master is a full-time job. It's hard to help the team when they need you the most if you're not even there!

In this particular instance, I was the visiting Scrum Master asked to observe. The conversation with the other Scrum Master didn't take place until after the Sprint Planning ended abruptly and with some hard feelings. In hindsight, I wish I had called for a break or whispered to my fellow Scrum Master to do this.

After we talked, the Scrum Master pulled the Developers back together later that day to revisit the Sprint Backlog and to ensure everyone was in agreement. Sure enough, another team member had come up with a solution for the item that everyone could agree on – even the two who had been conflicted earlier over their initial thoughts on how to turn the PBI into a valuable Product Increment.

At this point in our case studies, are you starting to pick up on the people skills effective Scrum Masters need to acquire? Or are you feeling like Cypher in *The Matrix* where he says:[16]

---

[16] Wachowski & Wachowski, *The Matrix*.

"I know what you're thinking, 'cause right now I'm thinking the same thing. Actually, I've been thinking it ever since I got here: why oh why didn't I take the BLUE pill?"

Chapter Nine

Case Study: Your Lack of Faith is Disturbing

You're a Certified ScrumMaster® and have even earned the Certified Scrum Professional® credential based on your work experience with Scrum. You have been hired at a new organization which is a joint venture between two companies to expand a service they created to a global market. The organization's Chief Information Officer (CIO) asks you to teach Scrum to everyone in the technology organization. The CIO has requested that the organization use Scrum going forward as a way to deliver business value more quickly than the traditional way of doing work. The organization is also distributed geographically and conducts work virtually.

This is an exciting opportunity for you: it's a chance to leverage all of your previous experiences in helping the participants learn how Scrum works and what typically leads to its failure. You set up a series of Scrum Fundamentals classes with about 25 people in each class. The first class that you will lead includes a number of the managers and directors as well as people doing the work.

The company believes that Scrum will enable them to achieve their goal of scaling their services globally. The project management process they are using, isn't delivering product as fast as leaders would like. They have identified a pilot team to do a proof of concept that consists primarily of people who have traditionally developed and tested the software solution that enables the business services to customers.

It's Day 1 of the first class. The participants are open to learning and are enjoying the exercises that you have prepared to demonstrate how cross-functional teams work together to produce results more quickly. Just before the lunch break, you begin talking about what Sprints are, what they produce and how Scrum recognizes no title other than Developer. Developers work together, conducting all activities cross-functionally to produce a working product increment.

Chapter Nine

You share the page in the official Scrum Guide where it's explained that Scrum recognizes no traditional titles such as: business analyst, programmer, tester, etc. Any team member can perform an activity, working with each other to achieve the Sprint Goal.

There is silence in the virtual room. You can tell that people are typing and don't know if they are sending chat messages to each other or if the silence and lack of questions or reactions mean they aren't engaged. You ask, "Who has a question about what I just explained?" This is met with more silence. "If there are no questions, do you want to move on to the next topic?"

The most senior person in the virtual room is a director within the organization. The director says, "We know that you're new to the organization. Did anyone explain to you by any chance the recent structural changes that we made?"

"I know in initial hiring conversations I was excited about the cross-functional structure. Is that the change you made prior to me starting?" you reply.

"No. That was our old structure. A few weeks ago, the CIO announced that in order for there to be more focus on quality, we would be restructuring the technology department by functionality. There is now a Business Analysis Team with a newly appointed functional manger. There is a Programming Team with a newly appointed functional manager and a Quality Assurance Team with a newly appointed functional manager," says the director. "This may have been in motion while you were being onboarded".

The new QA manager is also in the class and jumped in. "How am I supposed to accomplish the goals for my new team if they are loaned out to a different Scrum team? We were told that the QA team would use Scrum and lag a Sprint behind the programming team."

You pause. During the interview process, you had so carefully asked about the reasons why the organization was moving to Scrum and were pleased with the responses about delivering business value faster that you hadn't thought to ask about any plans to alter the structure that was in place at that time. You learned that there was no segregation by traditional functional role and didn't think there would be any reason for that to change given the organization's decision to adopt Scrum.

"Thank you for sharing that with me. There are no 'specialty Sprints' in Scrum. That means no Analysis

Chapter Nine

Sprint. No Programming Sprint. No Testing Sprint. Those are all activities to be completed during the Sprint by the cross-functional Developers who deliver increments of value," you explain.

"How do you see that being accomplished given the new structure?" asks the director.

"Well, that's an excellent question," you offer. "One that we won't be able to solve in a virtual training class without the appropriate decision-makers in the room who can affect a change. Let's start a backlog for the organization and as things come up that contradict moving to Scrum, we can take the items to the level of leadership to address them."

You continue the lesson on Sprints including that the very definition of a Sprint is delivery of a working product increment that could be shipped if the Product Owner decides to release it – not something that is partially done and not tested.

It's time to break for lunch and everyone agrees to reconvene in one hour. You can tell people are apprehensive and confused about how contradictory the new structure is to what you are teaching them. You grab lunch and hear your cell phone buzzing. You pick up and learn that it is the CIO giving you a call.

"What is this I'm hearing about you scaring the hell out of the people we asked you to train? I need you to stop that," the CIO says angrily.

"Excuse me? My apologies, but I'm not sure I understand how I am scaring them. I was asked to teach the technology group how Scrum works and that's what I'm doing," you reply.

"I just announced a re-organization and I am *not* changing it back to the way it was before," the CIO explains.

You reply: "The people seem confused. They understand the restructure but it appears to be aligned with a traditional way of doing work such as Waterfall or Project Management. Yet you are asking them to work this new way using Scrum that is based on cross-functional teams that is more in alignment with the way you used to be structured. So, they are left unsure of what it is the organization is really asking of them."

"Oh, you people and your Scrum religion, just stop it," the CIO says and hangs up the phone.

Chapter Nine

In response to the CIO's parting comment, you think to yourself, "Yes, I find your lack of faith disturbing."[17]

Problem Identification:

With many of the case studies, the root cause of the problem has come down to a people problem. That can occur at any level in an organization. In this scenario

---

[17] Lucas, G., (1977), *Star Wars Episode IV A New Hope*, Lucas Films; 20th Century Fox.

what would you do differently if *you* were the SM? Or what might you do next? Consider the following:

Agile Manifesto Values and Principles

- Principle #5: Build projects around motivated individuals. Give them the environment and the support they need, and trust them to get the job done.
- Principle #7: Working software is the primary measure of progress.
- Principle #11: The best architectures, requirements and designs emerge from self-organizing teams.
- Other applicable values and principles you can think of?

Scrum Guide

- The Scrum values of commitment, courage, focus, openness and respect.
- Within a Scrum Team, there are no sub-teams or hierarchies.
- Scrum Teams are cross-functional, meaning the members have all the skills necessary to create value each Sprint.
- The Scrum Team is responsible for all product-related activities from stakeholder collaboration, verification, maintenance, operation,

Chapter Nine

experimentation, research and development, and anything else that might be required.
- Developers are people in the Scrum Team that are committed to creating any aspect of a useable product increment each Sprint.
- The Scrum Master serves the organization coaching the organization in its Scrum adoption and removing barriers between stakeholders and the Scrum Team.
- Other Scrum Guide information you can think of that applies to this situation?

The Scrum Master in this scenario seemed to have done their due diligence during the interview process by asking questions regarding the organization's structure. They were so delighted in learning that there were no traditional component teams to break up into Scrum Teams, they stopped their line of questioning. An excellent additional question may have been to ask if the current structure would stay in place in rolling out Scrum or to find out what organizational leaders assume about Scrum.

The people doing the work in this scenario are saying very little. At least from what's presented in the case study. This doesn't always mean resistance. If people are confused or don't understand the change that is being proposed, sometimes it's assumed that they're "resisting" that change. The reality can be that they simply don't know what to change to – they are confused.

How about the newly appointed functional managers? What we don't know is much about the conversations that went into making those decisions other than "focus on quality". There are many Agile practices that focus on quality that have nothing to do with having one named role, one named department or a specific functional manager responsible for quality. In Scrum, quality is everyone's job. No one title equals a singular activity. Everyone can test and it is intended to happen as early as possible, not at the end of a development cycle.

Perhaps the biggest challenge in this case, is the CIO. Their sarcastic comment about "Scrum religion" reveals some negative assumptions they're making about the framework. What we don't know is why this is the case. If we put ourselves in this CIO's shoes for a moment, have they been asked by the main investor to use Scrum? This is a newly formed organization that is the joint venture of two powerful financial institutions. If we assume positive intent and think about the few facts that we know, it's just unknown who made the decision to use Scrum and who thinks it can deliver

Chapter Nine

business value any faster by misusing the framework on top of component team structures. Maybe the CIO made the decision. Maybe the decision was made above the CIO and they are struggling to work within contradictory messages just as much as their people are struggling.

What is known, is that Scrum requires structural change and behavioral change. What is needed in this situation is to get to the bottom of the contradictory directions: use Scrum to deliver value faster but structure by component promoting hand-offs and delays.

Possible Solutions:

The next step for this Scrum Master is to:
- Finish the training agreed to with the participants and continue noting any additional contradictions to using the framework that are identified
- Get on the CIO's calendar for a one-on-one conversation
- In advance of the conversation, it may be helpful to send the list of items identified by the participants in the Scrum training as contradictory to organizational structure, procedures, policies, etc.

- Recalling the Scrum values of Courage and Respect, it's probably a good idea for the Scrum Master to prepare a list of questions to ask in a non-judgmental way
- Depending on the outcome of the conversation, the CIO and Scrum Master can decide what to do next

The Scrum Master's initial response to the CIO may have come across as judgmental. Taking time to prepare curious questions about where the decisions originated to change the structure to adopt component teams and then to also change the way the work is done by using Scrum will be helpful to determine next steps.

Since the Scrum Master also serves the greater organization on the Scrum Team's behalf, the Scrum Master can offer to neutrally facilitate a leadership conversation with any additional people that the CIO identifies in answering the questions. It's crucial for the leaders to be on the same page in order to avoid confusing people who are asked to meet the company goals and objectives.

There may also be some perception about failing or about admitting to mistakes – either in decision-making or in communications. This is an opportunity for the Scrum Master to help these leaders understand that people will respect that level of honesty and transparency if admitting to any sort of mistake is ultimately what comes out of the leadership conversations.

Evaluation:

When you initially read the scenario, what did you focus on? There are myths that many new to Scrum believe to be true. Such as the myth of "specialty sprints". Or that teams of segregated activities just become sprints that "lag behind". This is one of those Waterfall Hangovers. It's the old mindset misusing the new vocabulary and framework. Scrum requires structural change and behavioral change.

Yet others who read this scenario will assume the Scrum Master should not be engaging in a conversation with the CIO, misunderstanding one-third of the job. The Scrum Master is a true leader who serves not only the Developers, the Product Owner but the greater organization on the Scrum Team's behalf. The Scrum Master also has the responsibility of coaching the organization on its Scrum adoption. Some organizations rush to train their people on Scrum which results in them reading the free, official Scrum Guide, yet those very leaders are operating on myths about the framework and haven't read the guide for themselves. The Scrum Guide is clear that no other roles are observed other than Developer and all skills must exist on the cross-functional Scrum Team in order to produce a working product increment with each Sprint.

In this particular instance, I was the Scrum Master delivering the training and engaged with the organization to help them adopt Scrum. The conversation with the CIO and the other leaders didn't go well. They firmly believed in the component team structure and I was told to make each component team a Scrum Team and to make that work. No amount of pointing out the contradictions to the Scrum framework or the conflicting directions made any difference to this leader. They were unwilling to read the Scrum Guide. They would also make comments about the flexibility of Agile must mean that they can change it to what they need it to be. The CIO chose to march forward with their plan. I chose to disengage with the organization instead of trying to follow it.

While I don't know what else transpired between the two investing companies in this venture after I left, one backed out a little over a year later and the newly formed company was dissolved shortly thereafter.

Chapter Nine

As I reflect on how the CIO behaved in this scenario, I'm reminded by what the Oracle says to Neo in *The Matrix Reloaded*:[18]

Oracle: "We can never see past the choices we don't understand."

---

[18] Wachowski, L., et al. (2003). *The Matrix Reloaded*, Warner Bros.

Chapter Ten

Case Study: Pardon my French

You're a Certified Scrum Professional®-SM newly hired by a company at the beginning of their Scrum adoption. Based on your years of experience working as a Scrum Master, you are excited to leverage the skills acquired in the CSP®-SM program. One of these things is planning the launch of a new Scrum Team.

The company likes your willingness to teach the Scrum framework as other Scrum Master candidates they talked to were hesitant to do this ... especially in a company that works virtually, in a distributed structure. You'll be the Scrum Master but are aware that the Scrum Guide describes the role as someone who not only coaches but trains as needed. You roll up your sleeves and hold training sessions to teach the Scrum framework as well as schedule Scrum Events including

Chapter Ten

Refinement conversations so that there's enough of a Product Backlog ready to get the Developers working in Sprints. Prior to this experience, no member of the Scrum Team had worked with any Agile method at this company or at any previous employers.

The leaders are pleased with the first handful of Sprints and really like the transparency of the Sprint Reviews, as this enables them to see exactly where new product development is at and to discuss what will come next with the Product Owner. They especially like that you and the Product Owner have worked to have these Sprint Reviews recorded in case some of them cannot attend "live". With several Sprints completed, the Developers seems to be adapting well to timeboxing, to the Scrum Events and to working together in a distributed, virtual way.

Sprint Planning is in full swing and the Developers are in agreement with the Product Owner on the Sprint Goal. Product Backlog Items (PBIs) that are needed to meet the goal are pulled onto the Sprint Backlog. With the first two parts of planning complete, the Product Owner leaves, saying that if any further questions arise, they should make contact via Instant Messenger or phone.

The Developers begin discussing how to accomplish the Sprint Goal by breaking PBIs into tasks. There are two members of the team who are very senior in their technical abilities and tend to be natural leaders. When they get along and work together, life for everyone is pretty good and things seem to flow nicely.

When they differ in technical opinion, however, there is a clash of the titans and work grinds to a halt while they argue and jockey for power or to try to win the argument. Today is one of those days.

One of the Developers is lobbying for a particular solution to a PBI discussed with the Product Owner. This team member assures the others that this is the most brilliant and efficient way to deliver what the users want.

Another Developer lobbies for a slightly different approach maintaining that there are several factors overlooked in the initially proposed solution and continues to request that the Product Owner be called back into the conversation to weigh in on the two approaches.

The team members argue with tensions mounting and they resort to swearing at each other including

Chapter Ten

calling each other profane names. You are very uncomfortable with this level of confrontation, and in particular, with the profanity. The team members are using language you consider inappropriate and you don't wish to condone such behavior. When the name calling starts, you sign off of the video call.

Problem Identification:

Regardless of the root cause for this particular situation, what are your thoughts about the Scrum Master choosing to just leave the video call? There are a number of things that need addressing here but first and foremost is the Scrum Master. In this scenario what would you do differently if *you* were the SM? And what might you do next? Consider the following:

Agile Manifesto Values and Principles

- Value: Individuals and Interactions over Processes and Tools.
- Principle #5: Build projects around motivated individuals. Give them the environment and the support they need, and trust them to get the job done.
- Principle #7: Working software is the primary measure of progress.

The Scrum Master Files

- Principle #10: Simplicity – the art of maximizing the amount of work not done – is essential.
- Principle #11: The best architectures, requirements and designs emerge from self-organizing teams.
- Other applicable values and principles you can think of?

Scrum Guide

- The Scrum values of commitment, courage, focus, openness and respect.
- These values give direction to the Scrum Team with regard to their work, actions, and behavior.
- The Scrum Team is self-managing, meaning they internally decide who does what, when and how.
- No one tells the Developers how to turn Product Backlog Items into increments of value.
- The Scrum Master coaches the team members in self-management and cross-functionality.
- The Scrum Master ensures that all Scrum Events take place and are positive, productive, and kept within the timebox.
- Other Scrum Guide information you can think of that applies to this situation?

The Developers and Product Owner are new to Scrum. Although the Scrum Master in this scenario is

Chapter Ten

not new to Scrum, they seem to be focusing solely on the elements of the framework: Sprint Planning, Refinement, Daily Scrum, Sprint Review and Sprint Retrospective. Scrum is also about demonstrating the values of Commitment, Openness, Focus, Respect and Courage and teamwork.

As a Scrum Team matures with the mechanics, what is often exposed are the people and organizational impediments. Effectively coaching through these items is the greater part of any Scrum Master's job and is often overlooked. When the swearing started, the Scrum Master chose to leave based on how they feel about profanity. Hence the title "Pardon my French" – a common phrase in the English language used by those who want their profanity use to be overlooked by others.

The Scrum Master Files

Although this Scrum Master has achieved the Certified Scrum Professional® level in their Scrum Mastery, they are missing nuanced aspects of the framework. This scenario is less about mechanics or technical solutions and is more about people.

What does it say to the Developers that the Scrum Master chose to leave at a time when an objective facilitator was needed the most? What about the other

Chapter Ten

members of the team? While two people are clearly disagreeing in an unhealthy way, what is the opinion of the other Developers? These matter also.

In the initial training and formation of the Scrum Team, was a working agreement created? It's not noted in the case study and when the argument broke out, nobody referred to such an agreement which could indicate that there is no such agreement in place. Even if there is no working agreement created by this team, at a minimum they would have learned the Scrum values: Openness, Commitment, Focus Respect and Courage. There seems to be no problem with Openness and Courage by two of the Developers but no Respect being demonstrated to each other or to the other people present.

The Scrum Guide indicates that the Scrum Master is responsible for not only timeboxing events but ensuring that they are productive and are positive. This Sprint Planning event seems to have taken a very negative turn at the point where the story ends.

Possible Solutions:

The first step is for the Scrum Master to realize that a servant leader would not have abandoned the team when help was needed most. The Scrum Master ideally would rejoin the session. Solving the root cause of this people issue will take time, but the Scrum Master could easily call for a break to ease the tension and give people a chance to cool off.

Upon returning to this Topic Three of Sprint Planning, the Scrum Master could avoid having everyone fall right back into the argument that was underway by asking for the other team members to weigh in. Scrum is about the Developers working together, not about everyone taking direction from a few people.

Based on what the other team members have to say, maybe the group decides which solution is the best one to move forward with given the discussion. Maybe one of them comes up with an even better solution than the two that were initially being debated. Without engaging the other Developers, we just don't know what the outcome there could be. It's up to the Scrum Master as the objective facilitator to help them work through this.

The Scrum Master could even use a Pros vs Cons visual facilitation on a virtual whiteboard or in a virtual collaboration tool. They could also call for a vote by the Developers. Calling for a vote though, assumes that

Chapter Ten

there is an agreement in place about decision making such as the group will move forward with a "majority rules" vote or that there is a tie-breaking mechanism if there is an even number of people and there is a tied vote.

If it's decided that more information is needed from the Product Owner to best decide, the PO did say they were available. Someone would just need to call them back into the conversation. It's not a great idea to have the Product Owner decide which solution to move forward with as this takes away the Developers empowerment and ultimately their accountability. That's not to say that more discussion with the Product Owner on what the users want and don't want wouldn't be helpful. It may be just what some of the team members need to weigh in with their vote.

Newer Scrum Masters tend to focus on the mechanics of Scrum such as the parts of Sprint Planning or Sprint Review and the Sprint Retrospective. What all great Scrum Masters embrace is the people side of the job. In this case, the Scrum Master can set aside time or use the Sprint Retrospective to facilitate creation of a working agreement. This can include tactical things such as decision making but also behavioral things such as it's not ok to swear at each other.

Beyond these steps, it's probably a good idea for this Scrum Master to get to know people individually to best get to the bottom of why the relationship between two of the Developers is up one minute and down the next. This requires investing in some one-on-one conversations, maybe some paired conversations ... Scrum Masters work behind the scenes in addition to in the events. These also don't have to be formal. They can be a coffee conversation, yes even if it's two people grabbing a coffee or tea and hopping on a video call with each other.

The next steps for this Scrum Master are to:
- Rejoin the session and apologize for leaving
- Call for a break so everyone can step away for a bit and collect their thoughts
- Actively facilitate the remainder of Sprint Planning ensuring that the Developers agree on solutions for the Sprint Goal – asking the Product Owner to return if necessary
- Facilitate the creation of a working agreement with the Scrum Team
- Continue to lead by example enacting the Scrum values and working with team members collectively

Chapter Ten

but also individually on growing their skills and their teamwork

Evaluation:

When you initially read the scenario, what did you focus on? Those unfamiliar with the Scrum Guide will somehow think that the Product Owner leaving for Topic Three of Sprint Planning was "wrong". Product Owners don't dictate solutions to the Developers. The Developers decide how to turn the Product Backlog Items into working product increments. Don't forget items are discussed prior to Sprint Planning during Refinement. They were discussed again during Topic One and Topic Two of Sprint Planning. If Developers continually look to a Product Owner to dictate solutions to them, it sets up even more dysfunction and lack of accountability.

Yet others who read this scenario will agree with the Scrum Master's choice to leave. This choice isn't serving the Scrum Team or the Organization. The choice to leave is putting the focus on the Scrum Master and making it all about them. Which is the opposite of a servant leadership mindset. If the Scrum Master is uncomfortable or finds the behavior disrespectful, others probably do also. What a great opportunity to find out and take the attention off the two fighting and ask the other Developers how they are feeling or to weigh in. And as mentioned in the Possible Solutions, never underestimate the power of a break for everyone.

In the absence of some type of working agreement, there really is no team. There may be a collection of people assigned to a product or project – but without care and nurturing, they may never truly become a team. The power of the Scrum Team identifying what goes into the agreement is that they are more likely to abide by it. When a Scrum Master calls out a violation of any of those agreements going forward then, it's not personal, it's just a reminder or an observation of what is happening…which is what all great coaches do.

Scrum Masters are the coach to the Product Owner, the Developers and to the Organization on the Scrum Team's behalf. But when that Scrum Master doesn't understand coaching yet, who is coaching the coach? This doesn't mean telling them what to do or creating artificial hierarchies that are not intended within an organization or outside of it.

In this particular instance, the Scrum Master had engaged me as a coach personally - the company was

Chapter Ten

not paying for the sessions. When this scenario was shared with me several sessions into our engagement, the Scrum Master sought my approval even phrasing their question as a leading one: "I did the right thing by leaving didn't I, Coach"?

When I disagreed and began asking this Scrum Master questions to assist them with self-reflection, it was obvious they had stopped listening and had checked out. They wanted there to be a "right" answer and for their decision to be validated. As a result, this was our last coaching session. None of us can change another person. We can only change ourselves. I could have engaged in powerful questions sooner as a way for this Scrum Master to self-reflect on their own choices in the situation.

As I recall this coaching conversation, I'm reminded by what the Oracle says to Morpheus in *The Matrix Revolutions (2003):* [19]

Morpheus: *"After everything that has happened, how can you expect me to believe you?"*
The Oracle: *"I don't. I expect just what I've always expected: For you to make up your own damn mind. Believe me or don't."*

---

[19] Wachowski, L., et al. (2003). *The Matrix Revolutions*, Warner Bros.

The Scrum Master Files

Chapter Eleven

Final Secrets

When I was a naïve Scrum Master, there were many things that I thought I knew about Scrum. The reality is that I was approaching the work the same old project management way and misusing the mechanisms in the Scrum framework to fit into project management. This doesn't make me a bad Scrum Master; it didn't make me a good one either. It wasn't about doing Scrum right or the fact that we were doing Scrum wrong. It's not about that at all! It's about delivering value to customers.

As a result, we weren't failing for new reasons. Missed deadlines, unhappy customers and crappy products coming out of a project management process in which we'd slapped Scrummy vocabulary on old habits, structures and behaviors was the problem. Scrum requires structural change and behavioral change.

I wasn't alone in my copying-without-knowledge. Many leaders of organizations do the exact same thing. They hear buzzwords and rush to be compliant with those words. They want to "go Agile" in the hopes of faster delivery but spend little time getting educated on what Agile means. They also skip the very crucial steps about identifying customers and products so that structure change can deliver value to those customers more readily.

The Scrum Master has responsibilities to coach the organization on its Scrum adoption. So, if the Scrum Master doesn't understand Scrum, it's unlikely that the leaders in the organization are being coached on Scrum. Please don't get me started on bringing in an "Agile Coach". That may sound odd coming from someone who offers that service. If you have chosen Scrum as the way to do work, and the Scrum Master needs temporary guidance, a coach could help. Please go back and read that sentence again. Temporary. There's no need for a Scrum Master **and** an Agile Coach if the Scrum Master is performing the role as intended. Why would you pay two people to do the job of one?

Recall there is also no hierarchy in a Scrum Team. That means an Agile Coach does not need to be added so that there's a hierarchy for Scrum Masters to report to. Scrum doesn't prescribe how to structure a company. Guess what? Neither does the Project Management Body of Knowledge®. Your company has the structure that it has because someone chose it. Someone chose to put in policies, procedures and structures to support its chosen way of doing work. If it now wants to change the way that work is done, then there needs to be a conversation about what structural changes are needed to support that. The most effective Scrum adoptions that I have the privilege of no longer coaching, always have the Scrum Master reporting to the highest level to tackle impediments. Yes, that means in some companies who no longer need me, the Scrum Master reports to a CEO, a CIO or a COO.

If You're Sprinting, You're Spending

Damaging, common myths and anti-patterns in Scrum adoptions include:
- Thinking there's a Sprint 0
- Believing an "Agile tool" is needed to do work
- Telling people that they have to use User Stories and Story Points to "do Scrum"
- Hybrids are needed because you can't show a date, scope or budget in Scrum

The Scrum Master Files

By definition a Sprint produces a working product increment that could be shipped if the Product Owner wants to release it. There's no Sprint 0, Design Sprint, Coding Sprint, Testing Sprint, etc. That's the waterfall mindset and behavior misusing Scrummy language. Recall that Scrum Teams have all of the skills needed cross-functionally to produce a working product increment or increments in a timebox called a Sprint.

Chapter Eleven

Enough Refinement needs to occur before a Sprint begins and then it's the responsibility of the Product Owner to stay ahead of the Developers in the ongoing activity of Refinement. If it's decided that an item for the product isn't going to be pursued in Refinement with subject matter experts and stakeholders, the PO doesn't need to bring it to the Developers. The Product Owner's responsibility is to bring ready items to the team in an ongoing manner. That means that the PO must continually be refining with customers, stakeholders, subject matter experts, etc. prior to engaging the Developers for further refinement.

Doing Refinement as "big up-front planning" is again a waterfall mindset misusing Scrummy words. Please don't take that as bad or good or right or wrong. The reality is that it costs time and money. It's people guessing. They will never guess right. If they were that clairvoyant they wouldn't need to work for a living. Guesses do not equal commitment.

Then when they do start "sprinting", things change. That's the only constant. Big, up front planning is time and money that is wasted and you can't get it back. Transparency, Inspect, Adapt. If the Waterfall Hangover is strong, people may have forgotten that we get to work and adapt. Change happens. Making it

Transparent so that we can Inspect and then decide how to act - to Adapt - is the empirical nature of the Scrum framework. The only thing that gives us answers is getting to work ... not spending time guessing.

Processes exist within the Scrum framework but those are solely decided upon by the Scrum Team. Processes are inherent to the product being built. One process won't work for one product yet might for another. It kills an organization's agility from the start when a software tool dictates process to everyone. Isn't it ironic that the very first value in the "Agile" Manifesto is "Individuals and Interactions over Processes and Tools"? Enterprise agile software tools *are* prescribing processes and tools and ignoring the individuals and interactions part of that phrase.

Telling people to write user stories and estimate in story points also appear nowhere in the Scrum framework. The creators of the User Story intended for the human, the user to tell their story. They tell the story to the people doing the work who capture what they heard so there's no lost in translation. If you have people writing down user stories and handing those documents or stories off to other people who now have to read and interpret them, congratulations! That sounds an awful lot like business requirements being

Chapter Eleven

documented and being handed off and skipping the conversation. Misusing more Agile ideas to preserve waterfall behavior. If you don't believe that the written word is misinterpreted let's look at your own experiences. Have you ever misunderstood an email? Directions? A recipe? The whole point with user stories is the conversation. Why do we try so hard to skip that and replace it with documents?

User Stories to capture Product Backlog Items in Scrum isn't wrong. It isn't right either. The Product Owner is the person who gets to determine how the Product Backlog is managed. If they don't want to use User Stories, they don't have to. If they are being told they have to, now we're getting into more dysfunctions by disrespecting the Product Owner's authority. According to the Scrum Guide their decisions are respected. Their decisions are not overturned.

Telling Developers that they have to size Product Backlog Items in story points is also disempowering them. It's their decision how work is sized. Maybe they want to size in T-Shirt sizes, maybe they want to use zoo animals to size work. It's solely their decision. If they are told they have to use story points, not only are they being disempowered and disrespected, don't be surprised when they aren't bought into the decision.

Their accountability has been taken away with prescription that isn't intended in this framework.

Product Owners are responsible for showing stakeholders where things are at with scope, timelines and budget. It's not that these things can't be provided in Scrum … they can be provided. It requires keeping a consistent team, a consistent sprint cadence and consistent sizing method within the Scrum Team.

A Scrum Master coaches the PO on effectively providing this stakeholder information and helps the stakeholders understand we can get information on these items at the end of every Sprint at the Sprint Review. Not only are those forecasts far simpler to create with the consistent team and sprints, but they are based on data. The data is based on Sprints complete. Actual history. If you completed a Sprint, there is work done and money spent. Forecasts in Scrum aren't based on guesses. But this requires "using as intended". If we start throwing in contradictory practices from other methods and confusing everyone, side effects are likely to occur.

Chapter Eleven

If You Can't Scrum, You Can't Scale

Why doesn't this book include any chapters on "scaling" Scrum? Because the reality is this: if you can't Scrum, you can't scale. Agile and Scrum have become big business for many companies. There are far more confusing choices on the menu that have the word scaling in them. They aren't likely to produce value to your customers any more readily than project management if they allow for component teams of specialists.

Your company is optimized for the results it's getting. If you want different results, that requires change. Doing work differently. Having singular activities segregated in one component team promotes hand-offs, waiting, and waste. There's nothing like that described in Scrum. Hence the phrase *if you can't Scrum you can't scale*. If your organization isn't making the necessary structural changes, they aren't ready to take what they're doing to a larger scale. All that is likely to happen is that the dysfunctions they're seeing with what they're calling Scrum will only be magnified and made that much more obvious and painful at "scale".

The first step is agreeing on who the customers are and what the products are. Then the organization needs to agree on aligning structurally to be able to deliver valuable product to those customers. If this happens, your company may be ready to scale. If what you are calling "product" isn't being sold to someone external to the company (the customer), you are likely misidentifying the product.

If that doesn't seem practical given how far the company chose to go with segregating activities, physical environments and putting "the system" as priority before the paying customers, there are ways to get started. It requires having an understanding of what the organization's goal is with scaling, a clear path to make changes and a commitment to continuously improving.

Scaling is considered an advanced concept. Training and information are available on the various choices that also exist in the market. Companies have to decide how much change they are willing to make before deciding which scaling method to adopt or where to start. The risk in choosing a practical place to start is forgetting about continuous improvement. What if the practical place to start becomes the new status quo and continuously improving stops?

Chapter Eleven

Your Ego is not Your Amigo!

Every one of us has an ego. It's a small part inside the frontal lobe of the brain. This is our sense of self and consciousness. The ego streams thoughts to us all day long. These thoughts can be assumptions and judgements. If those assumptions are false or those judgements are not true, but we act as if they are, it's a recipe for misunderstandings.

An effective Scrum Master has to silence their own ego to be able to remain objective and to assist others in more effective communication and teamwork. This is something that will take continued practice. To help people silence their own ego and to focus on the work or action needed, try asking:
- "What could you/we do next that would help us move forward?"
- "Are we telling ourselves a story that isn't true?"
- "What are the facts of the situation?"

This will also require a Scrum Master to be actively listening and tuning into all the people "stuff" pointed out in the case studies. As an example, ask for clarification when you hear vague terms such as: "it", "they", "always", "everyone", "never", "nobody", etc.

Ask:
- "Why are we doing this work/ why is it important"
- "What is the goal / what problem are we trying to solve / what is the plan"
- "How will we meet the goal / how will we approach the work / how will you do it"
- "Who do you mean / who do we need / who needs to know"
- "When should we check in again / when is this work due / when is it expected"

I can't stress enough that getting out of ego takes practice. If you re-read this chapter and note the number of times that I have pointed out it's not about right or about wrong. Have you caught yourself thinking about your own organization? Has your ego said to you "We've been doing it all wrong"! That's an example of how powerful that inner voice can be. Despite best efforts to convey that changing the way you do work isn't about right or wrong, your ego may have assumed or judged the situation in those terms.

Recall that trip to visit the Oracle in the Wachowski's (1999) *The Matrix*:[20]

Neo: "…and she's never wrong."

---

[20] Wachowski, L., & Wachowski, L. (1999), *The Matrix*, Warner Bros.

Chapter Eleven

Morpheus: "Try not to think of it in terms of right and wrong. She is a guide, Neo. She can help you to find the path."

Further deposit due by 26 Nov 2023
TUI Holidays £350

~~Tinwhistle~~

Book 14/10
off
~~(Timothy) Where is he~~

Conclusion

The choice to share what I have learned in a book turned out very differently from where it started. This idea started with a desire to share a specific case study so that people could learn from it. In visiting that customer, a little over a year after my engagement with them, I had another "aha" moment. In challenging my ego, the new thoughts became: "this isn't about you"; "these are not choices you made"; "you pointed them in a direction but it's their choices that led them here".

In true empirical fashion from that moment, I inspected and adapted. I had also been looking naively at Agile, more specifically Scrum, in terms of "right" or "wrong" and it's not about that at all! Sometimes we are so conditioned to think that failure is a "bad" thing instead of a "good" thing that we don't take the first step. We don't try or even run the experiment. Which is contradictory to how human beings learn. Taking the first step and falling *is* how we learn to walk. Uttering the first sounds that make no sense to anyone else *is* how we learn to talk.

Chapter Twelve

My next attempt to write a book about why Scrum doesn't work didn't come to fruition either. That "aha" moment was that it's impossible to follow a recipe when implementing Scrum. It's impossible to follow a prescription with contextual things like customers, products and people and think the same result will be achieved. Look how many people foolishly try to copy companies like Spotify? The only difference between companies who say Scrum works and companies who say Scrum doesn't work is the choices they are making. A company may make a series of choices that result in poor products and unhappy customers. If that company learns from those choices and makes different ones that leads them to excellent products and happy customers – would they have gotten there without the initial failure?

Today I know that the secrets I shared with you in this book were the results of *my* early failures. I used to think of failure as a negative thing and today I know it's the greatest teacher. Think of F.A.I.L. as standing for First Attempt In Learning. So, third time is a charm to get these secrets into this book. Without my early stumbles as a recovering Project Manager and naïve Scrum Master, I would not understand the things that I do today. I would not have the successes with Scrum and Agile that I do today.

The Scrum Master Files

The case studies shared with you are intended to be an inspiration and teaching tools. That's why they needed to be completely anonymous! To allow you to focus on the important aspects of each story. While it's impossible to copy someone else's journey or someone else's experiences, there are lessons that can be learned in working through the scenarios.

Whichever way the wind blows for you or whatever path you choose with your agility, I hope that your first attempts in learning serve you well!

Chapter Twelve

Printed in Great Britain
by Amazon